Dissecting The
Hitler
Mind

By Walter C. Langer

Introduction by Michael Ford

Declassified Psychological Analysis of Adolf Hitler

Listen To Mein Kampf

Understanding Hitler

A new video documentary which explains how Hitler was able to rise to power and the part Mein Kampf played in his plan.

Find out more about this video at www.HitlerLibrary.org

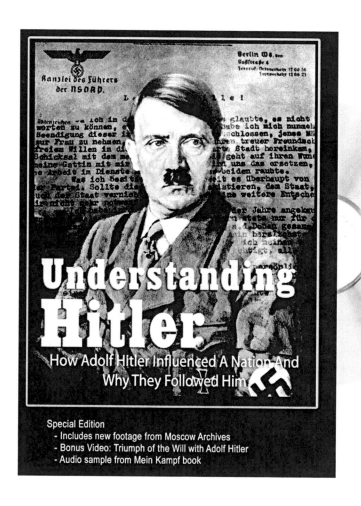

Introduction

The Office of Strategic Services was established in 1942 and headed by the infamous Colonel William J. Donovan, commonly known as Wild Bill Donovan. This new organization was the forerunner of the modern C.I.A and was intended to gather intelligence and organize psychological and propaganda warfare in preparation for war. The author of this report, Walter C. Langer, was a psychoanalyst who was known to Donovan. Donovan suggested a comprehensive psychological survey of Adolf Hitler be made which would help in their efforts.

During the research, Langer and other researchers interviewed individuals in the United States and Canada who had some contact with Hitler, as well as going through newspapers and books by those around Hitler. They eventually collected more than eleven thousand pages. *This material is included in The Hitler Source Book, which was appended to the original study. The numbers that appear in parentheses after references in the study refer to the page numbers where the original material can be found in The Hitler Source Book.*

Three psychoanalysts were chosen to review this material. Langer concedes that some of the conclusions were drawn based on analysis of interview materials and not direct observation or questioning which can never produce a complete profile.

Using the collected information, Langer probed Hitler's mysterious family background all the way into his sexual abnormalities, his extreme fear of death, Messiah complex, the meaning of his vegetarianism, and many other aspects of his personality. By using his years of experience working with psychiatric patients who demonstrated similar traits, Langer accurately predicted Hitler's increasing isolation, his frequent outbursts of anger, and the general deterioration of his mental condition... even his suicide.

The study was rushed to completion in eight months. It was declared Secret and remained locked away from the public for 25 years. It is believed only

30 copies were made. No one knows how widely this information was distributed before the war or if it was used at any political level as a basis for making decisions. It appears that the report was either not used or that it was not taken seriously.

There are some misspellings such as "untravelled" instead of "untraveled", and "worshipped" instead of "worshiped", however, the work was originally written on a typewriter and not a spell-checking word processor. These errors have been preserved as long as they did not distract from the meaning.

The analysis also drew heavily on Hitler's own work, Mein Kampf. This was the book he wrote, half in prison after the failed Beer Hall Putsch, and half after being released. In Mein Kampf, Hitler set down many of his theories about people, race, nations, and politics. He also described his childhood and his creation of the Nazi party. The new Ford translation of Mein Kampf is also available in an audio format for easy listening and his own words are an excellent source for information on who Hitler was. You can find more information on this version and listen to a free sample at

www.Mein-Kampf-Audio.com

and other information at www.Hitler-Library.org

If you truly want to understand the motivation behind Hitler, you should read his book or listen to the audio version at these websites. Only the Ford translation has correctly and accurately re-translated the original German language version of Mein Kampf. Older translations contained many errors and mis-translations so make sure you obtain the Ford translation. Unfortunately, this new and corrected version was not available to Langer at the time he compiled his psychological report on Hitler.

Keep in mind that this analysis was made before America's entry into World War II. It is amazing how many predictions came true, though not all. This report contains many psychological assertions which, when taken in one big lump, may incorrectly portray Hitler was a basket case of problems. This is not accurate and it is well known that Hitler acted rationally, strategically, and surgically, in many cases whether they be militarily, politically and personally. At least, this is true before the final years of his life.

We must also remember that the man Hitler became was not solely the result of unconscious Freudian psychological drives but also of rational decisions which he based on facts or ideas he had learned from various sources.

This report is sometimes improperly quoted in order to spread the inaccurate story that Hitler's grandmother, Maria Anna Schickelgruber, had an affair with a Jewish man who's house she worked in. This would have made Hitler's father half Jewish. This information was even reported to Hitler as a result of an investigation he ordered into his own past, however there is no evidence to support this claim and the source has since been discredited. However, the facts are less important than whether or not Hitler believed it might be true which is something that haunted him much of his life.

Since the report was published, more research has surfaced and more interviews, including those at the Nuremburg trials, has corrected a number of statements. Please keep this in mind when reading the report. We have not corrected any part of it to maintain the original integrity. In spite of this, the information in this report is amazingly accurate. That being said, there are a number of errors. For example, Hitler was not a heavy drinker but was not against an occasional beer. He even had a favorite low-alcoholic brew of choice. He did not have dirty fingernails and kept himself clean. He was actually obsessed with preventing bodily odors. He did not admire Franklin Roosevelt either.

Langer's predictions for Hitler's future were also astonishing in their accuracy. Langer offered one possibility of Hitler dying of natural causes. This was dismissed at the time because it was believed he was in good health, however it is now know that he had a number of health problems and these along with other phobias led him to take a long list of dangerous medicines which would have prevented him from living much longer than he did.

Langer's next prediction was for suicide and he said this was the most plausible end. This turned out to be exactly what happened. Overall, the analysis is surprisingly accurate and a valuable psychological glimpse into the mind of Adolf Hitler.

REPORT

The following Psychological Analysis of Adolf Hitler was compiled by the *Office Of Strategic Services* and was marked as Secret. It has been declassified and released to the public. This document has been retyped for easier reading but is exact in every other detail.

Records of the Central Intelligence Agency(Record Group 263)

– Special Authorization Section

ORIGINAL REPORT CREATED 1943

CLASSIFICATION ~~SECRET~~

CHANGED TO UNCLASSIFIED March 12, 1968

CONTENTS

A Psychological Analysis

of Adolf Hitler: His Life and Legend

by

Walter C. Langer

M. O. Branch
Office of Strategic Services
Washington, D. C.

With the collaboration of-
Prof. Henry A. Murray, Harvard
Psychological Clinic
Dr. Ernst Kris, New School for Social
Research
Dr. Bertram D. Lewin, New York
Psychoanalytic Institute

Preface

This study is not propagandistic in any sense of the term. It represents an attempt to screen the wealth of contradictory, conflicting and unreliable material concerning Hitler into strata which will be helpful to the policy-makers and those who wish to frame a counter-propaganda. For this reason the first three parts are purely descriptive and deal with the man (1) as he appears to himself, (2) as he has been pictured to the German people, and (3) how he is known to his associates. These sections contain the basic material for the psychological analysis in sections IV and V in which an attempt is made to understand Hitler as a person and the motivations underlying his actions.

The material available for such an analysis is extremely scant and spotty. Fortunately, we have at our disposal a number of informants who knew Hitler well and who have been willing to cooperate to the best of their abilities. The study would have been entirely impossible were it not for the fact that there is a relatively high degree of agreement in the descriptions of Hitler's behavior, sentiments and attitudes given by these several informants. With this as a basis it seemed worthwhile to proceed with the study filling in the lacunae with knowledge gained from clinical experience in dealing with individuals of a similar type. This is not an entirely satisfactory procedure, from a scientific point of view, but it is the only feasible method at the present time. Throughout the study we have tried to be as objective as possible in evaluating his strengths as well as his weaknesses.

All plain numbers in parentheses refer to the page of The Hitler Source Book, a companion volume in which the original material is to be found together with the complete reference. Numbers in parentheses preceded by M.K. or M.N.O. refer to pages in Mein Kampf and My New Order, respectively. A detailed Index to the original material is to be found at the beginning of the Source-Book. A complete bibliography is appended to this study.

It is hoped that the study may be helpful in gaining a deeper insight into Adolf Hitler and the German people and that it may serve as a guide for our propaganda activities as well as our future dealings with them.

Walter C. Langer

Consultant, M. O. Branch, OSS

Hitler
As he believes himself to be

At the time of the reoccupation of the Rhineland, Hitler made use of an extraordinary figure of speech in describing his own conduct. He said,

> "I follow my course with the precision and security of a sleepwalker."

Even at that time it struck the world as an unusual statement for the undisputed leader of 67,000,000 people to make at the time of an international crisis. Hitler meant it to be a form of' reassurance for his more wary followers who questioned the wisdom of his course. It seems, however, that it was a true confession and had his wary followers only realised its significance and implications they would have had grounds for far greater concern that that aroused by his proposal to reoccupy the Rhineland. For the course of this sleep-walker has carried him over many untravelled roads which finally led him unerringly to a pinnacle of success and power never reached before. And still it lured him on until today he stands on the brink of disaster. He will go down in history as the most worshipped and the most despised man the world has ever known.

Many people have stopped and asked themselves: "Is this man sincere in his undertakings or is he a fraud?" Certainly even a fragmentary knowledge of his past life warrants such a question, particularly since our correspondants have presented us with many conflicting views. At times, it seemed almost inconceivable that a man could be sincere and do what Hitler has done in the course of his career. And yet all of his former associates whom we have been able to contact, as well as many of our most capable foreign correspondents, are firmly convinced that Hitler actually does believe in his own greatness. Fuchs reports that Hitler said to Schuschnigg during the Berchtesgaden [name error in original] interviews:

> "Do you realize that you are in the presence of the greatest German of all time?"

It makes little difference for our purpose whether he actually spoke these words or not at this particular time as alleged. In this sentence he has summed up in a very few words an attitude which he has expressed to some of our informants in person. To Rauschning, for example, he once said:

> "Aber ich brauche sie nicht, um mir von ihnen meine geschichtiche Groesse bestaltigen zu lassen." (717)

And to Strasser, who once took the liberty of saying that we was afraid Hitler was mistaken, he said:

> "I cannot be mistaken. What I do and say is historical." (378)

many other such personal statements could be given. Oechaner has summed up his attitude in this respect very well in the following words:

> "He feels that no one ins German history is equipped as he is to bring the Germans to the position of supremacy which all German statesman have felt they deserved but were unable to achieve." (669)

This attitude is not confined to himself as a statesman. he also believes himself to be the greatest war lord as, for example, when he says to Raischning:

> "Ich spiele nicht Krieg. Ich lasse mich nicht von `Feldherrn' kommandieren. Den Krieg fushre ich.

Den engentlichen Zeitpunkt zum Angriff bestimme ich. Es gibt nur eine guenstigen. Ich warde auf ihm warten. Mit eisernor Entschlossenheit. Unc ich warde ihn nicht verpassen..." (701)

And it seems to be true that he has made a number of contributions to German offensive and defensive tactics and strategy. He believes himself to be an outstanding judge in legal matters and does not blush when he stands before the Reichstag, while speaking to the whole world, and says,

> "For the last twenty-four hours I was the supreme court of the German people." (255)

Then, too, he believes himself to be the greatest of all German architects and spends a great deal of his time in sketching new buildings and planning the remodeling of entire cities. In spite of the fact that he failed to pass the examinations for admission to the Art School he believes himself to be the only competent judge in all matters of art. A few years ago he appointed a committee of three to act as final judges on all matters of art, but when their verdicts did not please him he dismissed them and assumed their duties himself. It makes little difference whether the field be economics, education, foreign affairs, propaganda, movies, music or women's dress. In each and every field he believes himself to be an unquestioned authority.

He also prides himself on his hardness and brutality.

> "I am one of the hardest men Germany has had for decades, perhaps for centuries, equipped with the greatest authority of any German leader... but above all, I believe in my success. I believe in it unconditionally." (M.N.O. 871)

That belief in his own power actually borders on a feeling of omnipotence which he is not reluctant to display.

"Since the events of last year, his faith in his own genius, in his instinct, or as one might say, in his star, is boundless. Those who surround him are the first to admit that he now thinks himself infallible and invincible. That explains why he can no longer bear either criticism or contradiction. To contradict him is in his eyes a crime of 'lese majeste'; opposition to his plans, from whatever side it may come, is a definite sacrilege, to which the only reply is an immediate and striking display of his omnipotence." (French Yellow Book, 945)

Another diplomat reports a similar impression:

"When I first met him, his logic and sense of reality had impressed me, but as time went on he appeared to me to become more and more unreasonable and more and more convinced of his own infallibility and greatness ..." (Henderson, 129)

There seems, therefore, to be little room for doubt concerning Hitler's firm belief in his own greatness. We must now inquire into the sources of this belief. Almost all writers have attributed Hitler's confidence to the fact that he is a great believer in astrology and that he is constantly in touch with astrologers who advise him concerning his course of action. This is almost certainly untrue. All of our informants who have known Hitler rather intimately discard the idea as absurd. They all agree that nothing is more foreign to Hitler's personality than to seek help from outside sources of this type. The informant of the Dutch Legation holds a similar view. He says:

"Not only has the Fuehrer never had his horoscope cast, but he is in principle against horoscopes because he feels he might be unconsciously influenced by them." (655)

It is also indicative that Hitler, some time before the war, forbade the practice of fortune-telling and star-reading in Germany.

It is true that from the outside it looks as though Hitler might be acting under some guidance of this sort which gives him the feeling of conviction in his infalibility. These stories probably originated in the very early days of the Party. According to Strasser, during the early 1920's Hitler took regular lessons in speaking and in mass psychology from a man named Hamissen who was also a practicing astrologer and fortune-teller. He was an extremely clever individual who taught Hitler a great deal concerning the importance of staging meetings to obtain the greatest dramatic effect. As far as can be learned, he never had any particular interest in the movement or any say on what course it should follow. It is possible that Hanussen had some contact with a group of astrologers, referred-to by one von Wiegand, who were very active in Munich at this time. Through Hanussen Hitler too may have come in contact with this group, for von Wiegand writes:

> "When I first knew Adolph Hitler in Munich, in 1921 and 1922, he was in touch with a circle that believed firmly in the portents of the stars. There was much whispering of the coming of another Charlemagne and a new Reich. How far Hitler believed in these astrological forecasts and prophesies in those days I never could get out of Der Fuhrer. He neither denied nor affirmed belief. He was not averse, however, to making use of the forecasts to advance popular faith in himself and his then young and struggling movement."

It is quite possible that from these beginnings the myth of his associations with astrologers has grown.

Although Hitler has done considerable reading in a variety of fields of study, he does not in any way attribute his infallibility or omniscience to any intellectual endeavor on his part. On the contrary, he frowns on such sources when it comes to guiding the destiny of nations. His opinion of the intellect is, in fact, extremely low, for in various places he makes such statements as the following:

> "Of secondary importance is the training of mental abilities."

> "Over-educated people, stuffed with knowledge and intellect, but bare of any sound instincts."

> "These impudent rascals (intellectuals) who always know everything better than anybody else..."

> "The intellect has grown autocratic, and has become a disease of life."

Hitler's guide is something different entirely. It seems certain that Hitler believes that he has been sent Germany by Providence and that he has a particular mission to perform. He is probably not clear on the scope of this mission beyond the fact that he has been chosen to redeem the German people and reshape Europe. Just how this is to be accomplished is also rather vague in his mind, but this does not concern him greatly because an "inner voice" communicates to him the steps he is to take. This is the guide which leads him on his course with the precision and security of a sleep-walker.

> "I carry out the commands that Providence has laid upon me." (490)

> "No power on earth can shake the German Reich now, Divine Providence has willed it that I carry through the fulfillment of the Germanic task." (413)

> "But if the voice speaks, then I know the time

has come to act." (714)

It is this firm conviction that he has a mission and is under the guidance and protection of Providence which is responsible in large part for the contagious effect he has had on the German people.

Many people believe that this feeling of Destiny and mission have come to Hitler through his successes. This is probably false. Later in our study (Part V) we will try to show that Hitler has had this feeling for a great many years although it may not have become a conscious conviction until much later. In auy case it was forcing its way into consciousness during the war and has played a dominant role in his actions ever since. Mend (one of his comrades), for example, reports:

> "An eine eigenartige Propheseiung errinere ich mich noch in diesem Zusammenhag: Kurs vor Weihnachten (1915) auesserte er sich, dass wir noch vieles von ihm hoeren werden. Wir sollen nur abwarten, bis seine Zeit gekommen ist." (208)

Then, too, Hitler has reported several incidents during the war which proved to him that he was under Devine protection. The most startling of these is the following:

> "I was eating my dinner in a trench with several comrades. Suddenly a voice seemed to be saying to me, 'Get up and go over there.' It was so clear and insistent that I obeyed automatically, as if it had been a military order. I rose at once to my feet and walked twenty yards along the trench carrying my dinner in its tin can with me. Then I sat down to go on eating, my mind being once more at rest. Hardly had I done so when a flash and deafening report came from the part of the trench I had just left. A stray shell had burst over the group in which I had been sitting, and every member of it was

killed." (Price, 241)

Then, also, there was the vision he had while in hospital at Pasewalk suffering from blindness allegedly caused by gas:

> "Als ich im Bett lag kam mir der Gedanke, dass ich Deutschland befreien wuerde, dass ich es gross machen wuerde, und ich habe sofort gewusst, dass das verwirklicht werden wuerde." (429)

These experiences must later have fit in beautifully with the views of the Munich astrologers and it is possible that underneath Hitler felt that if there was any truth in their predictions they probably referred to him. But in those days he did not mention any connection between them or dwell on the Divine guidance he believed he possessed. Perhaps he felt that such claims at the beginning of the movement might hinder rather than help it. However, as von Wiegand has pointed out, he was not averse to making use of the forecasts to advance his own ends. At that time he was content with the role of a "drummer" who was heralding the coming of the real savior. Even then, however, the role of drummer was not as innocent or as insignificant in Hitler's mind as might be supposed. This was brought out in his testimony during the trial following the unsuccessful Beerhall Putsch of 1923. At that time he said:

> "Nehmem Sie die Ueberzeugung hin, dass ich die Erringung eines Ministerpostens nicht als erstrebenswert ansehe. Ich halte es eine grossen Mannes nicht fuer wuerdigeseinen Namen der Geschichte nur dadurch ueberliefern zu wollen, dasser Minister wird. Was mir vor Augen stand, das war vom ersten Tage tausendmal mehr: ich wollte der Zerbrecher der Marxismus werden. Ich werde die Ausfgabe loesen, und wenn ich sie loese, dann waere der Titel eines Ministers fuer mich eine Laecherlichkeit. Als

ihh zum ersten Mal vor Richard Wagners Grab
stand, da quoll mir des Herz ueber vor Stolz,
dass hier ein Mann ruht, der es sich verbeten
hat, hinaufzuschreiben: Hier ruht Geheimrat
Musikdirektor Excellenz Baron Richard von
Wagner. Ich war stolz darauf, dass dieser Mann
und so viele Maenner der deutschen Geschichte
sich damit begnuegten, ihren Namen der Nachwelt
zu ueberliefern, nicht ihren Titel. Nicht aus
Bescheidenheit wollte ich 'Trommler' sein.
Das ist des Hoechste, das andere ist eine
Kleinigkett."

After his stay in Landsberg Hitler no longer referred
to himself as the "drummer." Occasionally, he would
describe himself in the words of St. Matthew, "as a voice
crying in the wilderness", or as St. John the Baptist
whose duty was to hew a path for him who was to come and
lead the nation to power and glory. More frequently,
however, he referred to himself as "the Fuehrer", a name
chosen by Hess during their imprisonment. (901)

As time went on, it became clearer that he. was thinking
of himself as the Messiah and that it was he who was
destined to lead Germany to glory. His references to
the Bible became more frequent and the movement began
to take on a religious atmosphere. Comparisons between
Christ and himself became more numerous and found their
way into his conversation and speeches. For example, he
would say:

"When I came to Berlin a few weeks ago and
looked at the traffic in the Kurfuerstendamm,
the luxury, the perversion, the iniquity, the
wanton display, and the Jewish materialism
disgusted me so thoroughly, that I was almost
beside myself. I nearly imagined myself to be
Jesus Christ when He came to His Father's temple
and found it taken by the money-changers. I can
well imagine how He felt when He seized a whip
and scourged them out." (905)

During his speech, according to Hanfstangl, he swung his whip around violently as though to drive out the Jews and the forces of darkness, the enemies of Germany and German honor. Dietrich Eckart, who discovered Hitler as a possible leader and had witnessed this performance, said later, "When a man gets to the point of identifying himself with Jesus Christ, then he is ripe for an insane asylum." The identification in all this was not with Jesus Christ, the Crucified, but with Jesus Christ, the furious, lashing the crowds.

As a matter of fact, Hitler has very little admiration for Christ, the Crucified. Although he was brought up a Catholic, and received Communion, during the war, he severed his connection with the Church directly afterwards. This kind of Christ he considers soft and weak and unsuitable as a German Messiah.

The latter must be hard and brutal if he is to save Germany and lead it to its destiny.

> "My feeling as a Christian points me to my Lord and Saviour as a fighter. It points me to the man who once in loneliness, surrounded by only a few followers, recognized these Jews for what they were and summoned me to fight against them and who, God's truth! was greatest not as a sufferer but as a fighter. In boundless love, as a Christian and as a man, I read through the passage which tells us how the Lord rose at last in His might and seized the scourge to drive out of the Temple the brood of vipers and adders. How terrific was the fight for the world against the Jewish poison." (M.N.O. 26)

And to Rauschning he once referred to "the Jewish Christ-creed with its effeminate, pity-ethics".

It is not clear from the evidence whether the new State religion was part of Hitler's plan or whether developments were such that it became feasible. It is true that Rosenberg had long advocated such a move, but there is no evidence that Hitler was inclined to take such a drastic step until after he had come to power. It is possible that he felt he needed the power before he could initiate such a change, or it may be that his series of successes were so startling that the people spontaneously adopted a religious attitude towards him which made the move more or less obvious. In any case, he has accepted this God-like role without any hesitation or embarrassment.

White tells us that now when he is addressed with the salutation, "Heil Hitler, our Savior", he bows slightly at the compliment in the phrase - and believes it. (664) As time goes on, it becomes more and more certain that Hitler believes that he is really the "Chosen One" and that in his thinking he conceives of himself as a second Christ who has been sent to institute in the world a new system of values based on brutality and violence. He has fallen in love with the image of himself in this role and has surrounded himself with his own portraits.

His mission seems to lure him to still greater heights. Not content with the role of transitory savior it pushes him to higher goals - he must set the pattern for generations to come. Von Wiegand says:

> "In vital matters Hitler is far from unmindful
> of the name and record of success and failure
> he will leave to posterity." (493)

Nor is he content to allow these patterns to evolve in a natural way. In order to guarantee the future he feels that he alone can bind it to these principles. He believes, therefore, that he must become an immortal to the German people. Everything must be huge and befitting as a monument to the honor of Hitler. His idea of a permanent building is one which will endure at least a thousand years. His highways must be known as "Hitler Highways", and they must endure for l onger periods of time than the Napoleonic roads. He must always be doing the impossible and leaving his mark on the country. This is one of the ways in which he hopes to stay alive in the minds of the German people for generations to come.

It is alleged by many writers, among them Haffner (418), Huss (410) and Wagner (489) thath he has already drawn extensive plans for his own mausoleum. Our informants, who left Germany some time ago, are not in a position to verify these reports. They consider them well within the realm of possibility, however. This mausoleum is to be the mecca of Germany after his death. It is to be a tremendous monument about 700 feet high, with all the details worked out so that the greatest psychologicaI effect might be attained. It is also alleged that his first errand in Paris after the conquest in 1940 was a visit to the Dome des Invalides to study the monument to Napoleon. He found this lacking in many respects. For example, they had put him down in a hole which forced people to look down rather than high up.

> "I shall never make such a mistake," Hitler said suddenly. "I know how to keep my hold on people after I have passed on. I shall be the Fuehrer they look up at and go home to talk of and remember. My life shall not end in the mere form of death. It will, on the contrary, begin then." (410)

It was believed for a time that the Kehlstein had been originally built as an eternal mausoleum by Hitler. It seems, however, that if that was his original intention he has abandoned it in favor of something even more grandiose. Perhaps the Kehlstein was too inaccessible to enable large numbers of people to come and touch his tomb in order to become inspired. In any case, it seems that far more extravagant plans have been developed. His plan, if it is to be successful, needs constant emotional play on hysteric mass minds, and the more he can arrange the ways and means of achieving this, after he dies, the more assured he is of attaining his final goal.

"He is firmly convinced that the furious pace and the epochal age in which he lived and moved (he really is convinced that he is the motivating force and the moulder of that age) will terminate soon after his death, swinging the world by nature and inclination into a long span of digestive process marked by a sort of quiet inactivity. People in his `1000 year Reich' will build monuments to him and go around to touch and look at the things he has built, he thought. He said as much on that glorified visit of his to Rome in 1938, adding that a thousand years hence the greatness and not the ruins of his own time must intrigue the people of those far-away days. For, believe it or not, that is how the mind of this man Hitler projects itself without a blush over the centuries." (410)

There was also a time a few years ago when he spoke a good deal about retiring when his work was done. It was assumed that he would then take up his residence in Berchtesgaden and sit as God who guides the destinies of the Reich until he dies. In July, 1933, while visiting the Wagner family, he talked at length about getting old and complained bitterly that ten years of valuable time had been lost between the Beerhall Putsch in 1923 and his accession to power. This was all very regrettable since he predicted that it would take twenty-two years to get things in adequate shape so that he could turn them over to his successor. (936) It is supposed by some writers that during this period of retirement he would also write a book which would stand for eternity as a great bible of National Socialism. (3) This is all rather interesting in view of Roehm's statement made many years ago:

"Am liebsten taet er Heute schon in den Bergen sitzen und den lieben Gott spielen." (715)

A survey of all the evidence forces us to conclude that

Hitler believes himself destined to become an Immortal Hitler, chosen by God to be the New Deliverer of Germany and the Founder of a new social order for the world. He firmly believes this and is certain that in spite of all the trials and tribulations through which he must pass he will finally attain that goal. The one condition is that he follow the dictates of the inner voice which have guided and protected him in the past. This conviction is not rooted in the truth of the ideas he imparts but is based on the conviction of his own personal greatness. (146) Howard K. Smith makes an interesting observation:

> "I was convinced that of all the millions on whom the Hitler Myth had fastened itself, the most carried away was Adolph Hitler, himself." (290)

We will have occasion in Part V to examine the origins of this conviction and the role it plays in Hitler's psychological economy.

Hitler
As the German people know him

When we try to formulate a conception of Adolph Hitler as the German people know him we must not forget that their knowledge of him is limited by a controlled press. Many thousands of Germans have seen him in person, particularly in the past, and can use this experience as a basis for their individual conception of him.

Hitler, from a physical point of view, is not, however, a very imposing figure - certainly not the Platonic idea of a great, fighting Leader or the Deliverer of Germany and the creator of a New Reich. In height he is a little below average. His hips are wide and his shoulders relatively narrow. His muscles are flabby; his legs short, thin and spindly, the latter being hidden in the past by heavy boots and more recently by long trousers. He has a large torso and is hollow-chested to the point where it is said that he has his uniforms padded. From a physical point of view he could not pass the requirements to his own elite guard.

His dress, in the early days, was no more attractive. He frequently wore the Bavarian mountain costume of leather shorts with white shirt and suspenders. These were not always too clean and with his mouth full of brown, rotten teeth and his long dirty fingernails he presented rather a grotesque picture. (F. Wagner) At this time he also had a pointed beard, and his dark brown hair was parted in the middle and pasted down flat against his head with oil. Nor was his gait that of a soldier. "It was a very ladylike walk. Dainty little steps. Every few steps he cocked his right shoulder nervously, his left leg snapping up as he did so." (279)

He also had a tic in his face which caused the corner of his lips to curl upward. (485) When speaking he always dressed in a common-looking blue suit which robbed him of all distinctiveness. At the trial following the unsuccessful Beerhall Putsch Edgar Mowrer, who saw him for the first time, asked himself:

> "Was this provincial dandy, with his slick dark hair, his cutaway coat, his awkward gestures and glib tongue, the terrible rebel? He seemed for all the world like a travelling salesman for a clothing firm." (642)

Nor did he make a much better impression later on. Dorothy Thompson, upon her first meeting, described him in the following terms:

> "He is formless, almost faceless, a man whose countenance is a caricature, a man whose framework seems cartilaginous, without bones. He is inconsequent and voluble, ill poised,

and insecure. He is the very prototype of the little man." (307)

Smith (289) also found him "the apotheosis of the little man", funny looking, self-conscious and unsure of himself.

It may be supposed that this is only the judgment of American journalists who have a different standard of masculine beauty. However, while testifying as a witness in the-law court in 1923, Professor Max von Gruber of the University of Munich, and the most eminent eugenist in Germany, stated:

> "It was the first time I had seen Hitler close at hand. Face and head of inferior type, cross-breed; low receding forehead, ugly nose, broad cheekbones, little eyes, dark hair. Expression not of a man exercising authority in perfect self-command, but of raving excitement. At the end an expression of satisfied egotism." (575)

A great deal has been written about his eyes which have been described in terms of almost every color of the rainbow. As a matter of fact, they seem to be rather a bright blue - bordering on the violet. But it is not the color which has attracted people, but rather their depth and a glint which makes them appear to have a hypnotic quality. One finds stories like the following recurring over and over again in the literature. A policeman who is noted for his antipathy to the Nazi movement is sent to a Hitler meeting to maintain order. While standing at his post Hitler enters:

> "He gazed into the police officer's eye with that fatal hypnotizing and irresistable glare, which swept the poor officer right off his feet. Clicking to attention he confessed to me this morning: 'Since last night I am a National Socialist. Heil Hitler.'" (Fromm, 369)

These stories are not all from the Nazi propaganda agencies. Very reliable people, now in this country, have reported similar incidents among their own personal acquaintances. Even outstanding diplomats have commented on the nature of his eyes and the way in which he uses them when meeting people, often with disatrous effects.

Then there are the others, like Rauschning, who find his look staring and dead - lacking in brilliance and the sparkle of genuine animation. (257) We need not dwell on his eyes and their peculiar quality, however, since relatively few Germans have come in such close contact with him that they could be seriously affected by them.

Whatever effect Hitler's personal appearance may have had on the German people in the past, it is safe to assume that this has been greatly tempered by millions of posters, pasted in every conceivable place, which show the Fuehrer as a fairly good-looking individual with a very determined attitude. In addition, the press, news-reels, etc., are continually flooded with carefully prepared photographs showing Hitler at his very best. These have undoubtedly, in the course of time, blotted out any unfavorable impressions he may have created as a real person in the past. The physical Hitler most Germans know now is a fairly presentable individual.

The only other real contact the overwhelming majority of people have had with Hitler is through his voice. He was a tireless speaker and before he came to power would sometimes give as many as three or four speeches on the same day, often in different cities. Even his greatest opponents concede that he is the greatest orator that Germany has ever known. This is a great concession in view of the fact that the qualities of his voice are far from pleasant - many, in fact, find it distinctly unpleasant. It has a rasping-quality which often breaks into a shrill falsetto when he becomes aroused. Nor is it his diction which makes him a great orator. In the early days this was particularly bad. It was a conglomeration of high German with an Austrian dialect which Tschuppik

(517) describes as a "knoedlige Sprache". Nor was it the structure of his speeches which made him a great orator. On the whole, his speeches were sinfully long, badly structured and very repetitious. Some of them are positively painful to read but nevertheless, when he delivered them they had an extraordinary effect upon his audiences.

His power and fascination in speaking lay almost wholly in his ability to sense what a given audience wanted to hear and then to manipulate his theme in such a way that he would arouse the emotions of the crowd. Strasser says of this talent:

> "Hitler responds to the vibration of the human heart with the delicacy of a seismagraph... enabling him, with a certainty with which no conscious gift could endow him, to act as a loudspeaker proclaiming the most secret desires, the least permissible instincts, the sufferings and personal revolts of a whole nation." (576)

Before coming to power almost all of his speeches centered around the following three themes: (1) the treason of the November criminals; (2) the rule of the Marxists must be broken; and (3) the world domination of the Jews. No matter what topic was advertised for a given speech he almost invariably would wind up on one or more of these three themes. And yet people liked it and would attend one meeting after another to hear him speak. It was not, therefore, so much what he said that appealed to his audiences as how he said it.

Even in the early days Hitler was a showman with a great sense of the dramatic. Not only did he schedule his speeches late in the evening when his audience would be tired and their resistance lowered through natural causes, but he would always send an assistant ahead of time to make a short speech and warm the audience up. Storm-troopers always played an important role at these meetings and would line the aisle through which he would pass. At the psychological moment, Hitler would appear in the door in the back of the hall. Then with a small group behind him, he would march through the rows of S.A. men to reach the speaker's table. He never glanced to the right or to the left as he came down the aisle and became greatly annoyed if anyone tried to accost him or hampered his progress. Whenever possible he would have a band present and they would strike up a lively military march as he came down the aisle.

When he began to speak he usually manifested signs of nervousness. Usually he was unable to say anything of consequence until he had gotten the feel of his audience. On one occasion, Heiden (499) reports, he was so nervous that he could think of nothing to say. In order to do something he picked up the table and moved it around on the platform. Then suddenly he got the "feel" and was able to go on. Price (241) describes his speaking in the following way:

> "The beginning is slow and halting. Gradually be warms up when the spiritual atmosphere of the great crowd is engendered. For he responds to this metaphysical contact in such a way that each member of the multitude feels bound to him by an individual link of sympathy."

All of our informants report the slow start, waiting for the feel of the audience. As soon as he has found it, the tempo increases in smooth rhythm and volume until he is shouting at the climax. Through all this, the listener seems to identify himself with Hitler' s voice which becomes the voice of Germany.

This is all in keeping with Hitler's own conception of mass psychology as given in MEIN KAMPF where he says:

> "The psyche of the broad masses does not respond to anything weak or half-way. Like a woman, whose spiritual sensitiveness is determined less by abstract reason than by an indefinable emotional

longing for fulfilling power and who, for that reason, prefers to submit to the strong rather than the weakling - the mass, too, prefers the ruler to a pleader."

And Hitler let them have it. NEWSWEEK (572) reported:

"Women faint, when, with face purpled and contorted with effort, he blows forth his magic oratory."

Flanner (558) says:

"His oratory used to wilt his collar, unglue his forelock, glaze his eyes; he was like a man hypnotized, repeating himself into a frenzy."

Yeates-Brown (592) :

"He was a man transformed and possessed. We were in the presence of a miracle."

This fiery oratory was something new to the Germans and particulary to the slow-tongued, lower-class Bavarians. In Munich his shouting and gesturing was a spectacle men paid to see (216). It was not only his fiery oratory, however, that won the crowds to his cause. This was certainly something new, but far more important was the seriousness with which his words were spoken.

"Everyone of his words comes out charged with a powerful current of energy; at times it seems as if they are torn from the very heart of the man, causing him indescribable anguish." (Fry, 577)

"Leaning from the tribune, as if he were trying to impel his inner self into the consciousness of all these thousands, he was holding the masses and me with them under a hypnotic spell... It was clear that Hitler was feeling the exaltation of the emotional response now surging up toward him... His voice rising to passionate climaxes... his words were like a scourge. When he stopped speaking his chest was still heaving with emotion." (Ludecke, 164)

Many writers have commented upon his ability to hypnotize his audiences. Stanley High (455) reports:

> "When, at the climax, he sways from one side to the, other his listeners sway with him; when he leans forward they also lean forward and when he concludes they either are awed and silent or on their feet in a frenzy."

Unquestionably, as a speaker, he has had a powerful influence on the common run of German people. His meetings were always crowded and by the time he got through speaking he had completely numbed the critical faculties of his listeners to the point where they were willing to believe almost anything he said. He flattered them and cajoled them. He hurled accusations at them one moment and amused them the next by building up straw men which he promptly knocked down. His tongue was like a lash which whipped up the emotions of his audience. And somehow he always managed to say what the majority of the audience were already secretly thinking but could not verbalize. When the audience began to respond, it affected him in return. Before long, due to this reciprocal relationship, he and his audience became intoxicated with the emotional appeal of his oratory. (Strasser, 295)

It was this Hitler that the German people knew at first hand. Hitler, the fiery orator, who tirelessly rushed from one meeting to another, working himself to the point of exhaustion in their behalf. Hitler, whose heart and soul were in the Cause and who struggled endlessly against overwhelming odds and obstacles to open their eyes to the true state of affairs. Hitler, who could arouse their emotions and channelize them towards goals of national aggrandizement. Hitler the courageous, who dared to speak the truth and defy the national authorities as well as the international oppressors. It was a sincere Hitler that they knew, whose words burned into the most secret recesses of their minds and rebuked them for their own shortcomings. It was the Hitler who would lead them back to self-respect because he had faith in them.

This fundamental conception of Hitler made a beautiful foundation for a propaganda build-up. He was so convincing on the speaker's platform and appeared to be so sincere in what he said that the majority of his listeners were ready to believe almost anything good about him because they wanted to believe it. The Nazi propaganda agencies were not slow in making the most of their opportunities.

Hitler, himself, had provided an excellent background for a propaganda build-up. From the earliest days of his political career he had steadfastly refused to divulge anything about his personal life, past or present. To his most immediate associates he was, in reality, a man of mystery. There was no clearing away of unpleasant incidents to be done before the building-up process could begin. In fact, the more secrecy he maintained about his personal life the more curious his followers became. This was, indeed, fertile ground on which to build a myth or legend.

The Nazi propaganda machine devoted all its efforts to the task of portraying Hitler as something extra-human. Everything he did was written up in such a way that it portrayed his superlative character. If he does not eat meat, drink alcoholic beverages, or smoke, it is not due to the fact that he has some kind of inhibition or does it because he believes it will improve his health. Such things are not worthy of the Fuehrer. He abstains from these because he is following the example of the great German, Richard Wagner, or because he has discovered that it increases his energy and endurance to such a degree that he can give much more of himself to the creation of the new German Reich.

Such abstinence also indicates, according to the propaganda, that the Fuehrer is a person with tremendous will-power and self-discipline. Hitler himself fosters this conception, according to Hanfstangl, who, when someone asked him how he managed to give up these things, replied: "It is a matter of will. Once I make up my mind not to do a thing, I just don't do it. And once that decision is made, it is taken for always. Is that so wonderful?"

The same is true in the field of sex. As far as the German people know he has no sex life and this too is clothed, not as an abnormality, but as a great virtue. The Fuehrer is above human weaknesses of this sort and von Wiegand (494) tells us that he "has a profound contempt for the weakness in men for sex and the fools that it makes of them." Hanfstangl reports that Hitler frequently makes the statement that he will never marry a woman since Germany is his only bride. However, Hitler with his deep insight into human nature, appreciates these weaknesses in others and is tolerant of them. He does not even condemn them or forbid them among his closest associates.

He is also portrayed in the propaganda as the soul of kindliness and generosity. Endless stories that illustrate these virtues are found over and over again in the literature. Price (236) cites a typical example: an attractive young peasant girl tries to approach him but is prevented from doing so by the guards. She bursts into tears and Hitler, seeing her distress, inquires into the cause. She tells him that her fiance had been expelled from Austria for his Nazi principles and that he cannot find work and consequently they cannot get married. Hitler is deeply touched. He promises to find the young man a job and, in addition, completely furnishes a flat for them to live in, even down to a baby's cot. Every attempt is made to present him as extremely human, with a deep feeling for the problems of ordinary people.

A great many writers, both Nazi and anti-Nazi, have

written extensively about his great love for children and the Nazi press is certainly full of pictures showing Hitler in the company of little tots. It is alleged that when he is at Berchtesgaden he always has the children from the neighborhood visit him in the afternoon and that he serves them candy, ice cream, cake, etc. Phayre (225) says, "Never was there a middle-aged batchelor who so delighted in the company of children." Princess Olga reported that when she visited Hitler in Berlin and the topic of children came up during the conversation, Hitler's eyes filled with tears.

The Nazi press had made extremely good use of this and endless stories accompany the pictures. Likewise, a great deal is written about his fondness for animals, particularly dogs. Here again, there are numberless pictures to prove it is so. As far as dogs are concerned, the propaganda is probably fairly near the truth but it goes far beyond that point in other respects. One writer even went so far as to attribute his vegetarianism to his inability to tolerate the thought of animals being slaughtered for human consumption (405). Hitler is pictured as an "affable lord of the manor", full of gentleness, kindliness and helpfulness, or, as Oechsner puts it, he is the Great Comforter - father, husband, brother or son to every German who lacks or has lost such a relative (668).

Another trait which has received a great deal of comment in the propaganda build-up is Hitler's modesty and simplicity. His successes have never gone to his head. At bottom he is still the simple soul he was when he founded the Party and his greatest Joy is to be considered as "one of the boys".

As proof. of this they point to the fact that he has never sought a crown, that he never appears in gaudy uniforms or does a great deal of entertaining. Even after he came to power he continued to wear his old trench coat and slouch hat for a time and when he donned a uniform it was always that of a simple storm-trooper.

Much was written about his fondness for visits from early acquaintances and how he loved to sit down in the midst of his busy day in order to talk over old times. There was really nothing he liked better than to frequent his old haunts and meet old friends while he was in Munich, or to take part in their festivities. At heart he was still a worker and his interests were always with the working classes with whom he felt thoroughly at home.

Hitler is also a man of incredible energy and endurance. His day consists of sixteen and eighteen hours of uninterrupted work. He is absolutely tireless when it comes to working for Germany and its future welfare and no personal pleasures are permitted to interfere with the carrying out of his mission. The ordinary man in the street cannot imagine a human being in Hitler's position not taking advantage of his opportunity. He can only imagine himself in the same position revelling in luxuries and yet here is Hitler who scorns them all. His only conclusion is that Hitler is not an ordinary mortal.

Phillips (868) reports the case of a young Nazi who once confided to him: "I would die for Hitler, but I would not change places with Hitler. At least when I wake every morning I can say, "Hail Hitler!", but this man, he has no fun in life. No smoking, no drinking, no women! - only work, until he falls asleep at night!"

A great deal is made of Hitler's determination. It is pointed out over and over again that he never gives up once he has made up his mind to attain a particular goal. No matter how rough the road, he plods along in unswerving determination. Even though he receives serious set-backs and the situation appears to be hopeless, he never loses faith and always gets what he goes after. He refuses to be coerced into compromises of any sort and is always ready to assume the full responsibility for his actions. The great trials and tribulations through which the Party had to pass on its way to power are cited over and over again and all the credit is given to

Hitler and his fanatical faith in the future.

Even his refusal to permit ordinary scruples to get in his way is given as a sign of his greatness. The fact that he did not communicate with his family for over ten years becomes a great virtue since it meant a severe deprivation to the young man who was determined to make something of himself before he returned home!

A great deal of publicity has also been given to his breath of vision, ability to penetrate the future and his ability to organize both the Party and the country in preparation for obstacles they will have to overcome. According to the propagandists, Hitler is the soul of efficiency and has an extraordinary power of resolving conflicts and simplifying problems which have stumped all experts in the past. In fact, his infallibility and incorruptibility throughout are not only implied but openly stated in no uncertain terms.

He is also a person of great patience who would never spill a drop of human blood if it could possibly be avoided. Over and over again one hears of his great patience with the democracies, with Czechoslovakia and with Poland. But here, as in his private life, he never loses control of his emotions. Fundamentally, he is a man of peace who desires nothing quite so much as to be left alone to work out the destiny of Germany in a quiet and constructive manner. For he is a builder at heart and an artist, and these prove that the creative and constructive elements in his nature are predominant.

This does not mean, however, that he is a coward. On the contrary, he is a person of outstanding courage. His way of life is proof of this, as well as his enviable record during the last war. A great many stories about his decorations for bravery have been circulated and particularly for his outstanding heroism when he was awarded the Iron Cross first-class. The fact that the stories of his performance vary from one time to another does not seem to disturb the people in the least.

Fundamentally, according to the Nazi press, Hitler is a man of steel. He is well aware of his mission and no amount of persuasion, coercion, sacrifices or unpleasant duties can persuade him to alter his course. In the face of all sorts of disasters and disagreeable happenings and necessary measures, he never loses his nerve for a moment. But he not hard in human qualities. He places loyalty and justice as the two of the greatest virtues and observes them with scrupulous care.

Loyalty means so much to him that the inscription over his door at Berchtesgaden reads, "Meine Ehre heisst Treue". He is the acme of German honor and purity; the Resurrector of the German family and home. He is the greatest architect of all time; the greatest military genius in all history. He has an inexhaustible fount of knowledge. He is a man of action and the creator of new social values. He is indeed, according to the Nazi propaganda bureau, a paramount of all virtues. A few typical examples may illustrate the extent to which they are carried in their praise of him.

> "Zunaechst Hitler sebst: Hitler is der Mann ohne Kompromiss. Vor allem kennt er keinen Kompromiss mit sicht selbst. Er hat einen einsigen Gedanken, der ihn leitet: Deutschland wieder aufzurichten. Diese Idee verdraengt alles um ihn. Er kennt kein Privatlehen. Er kennt Familienleben ebensowenig, wie er ein Laster kennt. Er ist die Verkoerperung des nationalen Willens.

> "Die Ritterschaft eines heiligen Zieles, das sich kein Mensch hoeher steken kann: Deutschland!... Hitler... uberracht (durch) seine warme Liebenswuerdigkeit. Ueber die Ruhe und Kraft, die beinahe physisch von diesem Mann ausstraht. Man waechst in er Naehe dieses Menschen... Wie er auf alle Dinge reagiert!... Eisern warden die Zuege und die Worte fallen wie Bein... Der klassische Ernst, mit dem Hitler und seine um

den Fuehrer gescharten Mitarbeiter ihre Sendung nehmen, that in der Geschichte dieser Welt nur wenige Paralellen." Czech-Jochberg: Adolph Hitler und sein Stab, 1933. (861)

"... such in den privaten Dingen des Lebens Vorbildlichkeit und menschliche Groesse ... ob Hitler ... umbraust wird yore Jubelnden Zuruf der Strassenabeiter, oder aufgewuehlt und erschuettert am Lager seine ermordeten Kameraden steht, immer ist um ihn diese Hoheit und tiefste Menschlichkeit . . . dieset einzigartigen Perseonlichkeit . . . ein grosser und guter Mensch. Hitler ist ein universaler Geist. Es ist unmoeglich der Mannigfaltigkett seines Wesens mit 100 Aufnahmen gerecht zu werden. Auch auf diesen beiden Gebleten (Architecture and History) ist Hitler eine unangreifbare Autoritaet. Unsere Zeit wird diesen Ueberragenden vielleicht verehren und lieben, aber wird ihn nicht in seiner grossen Tief ermessen koennen." Hoffman: Hitler, wie ihn keiner kennt, 1932 (899)

"Hitler is a modest man - and the world needs modest men. Therefore the people love him. Like every good leader, he must be an efficient follower. He makes himself the humblest disciple of himself, the severest of all disciplinarians with himself. In fact, Hitler is a modern monk, with the three knots of Poverty, Chastity and Obedience tied in his invisible girdle. A zealot among zealots., He eats no meat, drinks no wine, does not smoke. I am told he takes for himself no salary but lives privately from the income of his book, `Mein Kampf' ... Surplus funds he turns back to the S.A. His work day consists of eighteen hours, usually, and he often falls asleap in the last hour of his work. There have been four woman in his life - but only to help him along with service and money . . . He once gave a lecture at Bayreuth on Wagner and `Deutsche Liedot' that astounded the musical critics and revealed him as a musical scholar of parts ... Sheer opportunism never lured him as much as the opportunity to preach his doctrines. His quality is Messianic; his spiritual trend is ascetic; his reaction is medieval ..." Phillips: Germany Today and Tomorrow. (868)

Hitler not only knows about all these writings but since he has always been the gutiding spirit in all German propaganda and usually plans the broad lines that are to be followed, it is safe to assume that he himself is responsible for the instigation and development of this mythical personality. When we look back over the development of this build-up we can see clearly that Hitler, from the very beginning, planned on making himself a mythological figure. He opens MEIN KAMPF with the following passage:

"In this little town on the river Inn, Bavarian by blood and Austrian by nationality, gilded by the light of German martyrdom, there lived, at the end of the '80's of the last century, my parents: the father a faithful civil servant, the mother devoting herself to the cares of the household and looking after her children with eternally the same loving kindness."

This is the classic way of beginning a fairy tale rather than a serious autobiography or a political treatise. In the very first sentence of the book he implies that Fate was already smiling on him at the time of his birth, for it reads:

"Today I consider it my good fortune that Fate designated Braunau on the Inn as the plaee of ay birth."

As soon as Hitler came to power new weapons for self-aggrandizement were put into the hands of the propagandists and they made good use of them. Unemployment dropped off rapidly, new and imposing buildings were erected with astounding rapidity.

The face of Germany was being lifted at an incredible speed. Hitler was keeping his promises; he was accomplishing the impossible. Every success in diplomacy, every social reform was heralded as world-shaking in its importance. And for each success, Hitler modestly accepted all the credit. It was always Hitler that did this, and Hitler who did that, provided these acts were spectacular and met with the approval of the public. If they happened to meet with disapproval, it was always one of his assistants who was to blame. Every effort was/made to cultivate the attitude that Hitler was infallible and was carrying through his mission of saving Germany.

It was not long before the German people were prepared to take the short step of seeing Hitler, not as a man, but as a Messiah of Germany. Public meetings and particularly the Nurnburg took on a religious atmosphere. All the stagings were designed to create a supernatural and religious attitude and Hitler's entry was more befitting a god than a man. In Berlin one of the large art shops on Unter dean Linden exhibited a large portrait of Hitler in the center of its display window. Hitler's portrait was entirely surrounded as though by a halo, with various copies of a painting of Christ (High, 453). Notes appeared in the press to the effect that, "Als er sprach, hoerte man den Mantel Gottes durch den Saal rauschen!" Ziemar reports that on the side of a hill in Odenwald, conspicuous as a waterfall, painted on white canvas were the black words:

"We   believe   in   Holy   Germany
Holy   Germany   is   Hitler!
We believe in Holy Hitler!!" (763)

Roberts reports:

"In Munich in the early autumn of 1936 I saw colored pictures of Hitler in the actual silver garments of the Knights of the Grail; but these were soon withdrawn. They gave the show away; they were too near the truth of Hitler's mentality." (876)

Teeling (585) writes that at the Nurnburg Nazi Party Rally in September, 1937, there was a huge photograph of Hitler underneath which was the inscription, "In the beginning was the Word . . .". He also says that the Mayor of Hamburg assured him, "We need no priest or parsons. We communicate direct with God through Adolph Hitler. He has many Christ-like qualities." Soon these sentiments were introduced by official circles. Rauschning (552) reports that the Party has adopted this creed:

"Wir alle glauben auf dieset Erde an Adolph Hitler, unseren Fuehrer, und wir bekennen, dass der Nationalsozialismus der allein seligmachende Glaube fuer unser Volk ist."

A Rhenish group of German "Christians" in April, 1957, passed this resolution:

"Hitler's word is God's law, the decrees and laws which represent it possess divine authority." (550)

And Reichsminister for Church Affairs, Hans Kerrl, says:

"There has arisen a new authority as to what Christ and Christianity really are - that is Adolph Hitler. Adolph Hitler ... is the true Holy Ghost." (749)

This is the way Hitler hopes to pave his path to immortality. It has been carefully planned and consistently executed in a step by step fashion. The Hitler the German people know is fundamentally the fiery orator who fascinated them and this has gradually been embroidered by the propaganda until he lie now presented to them as a full-fledged deity. Everything else is carefully concealed from them as a whole. How many Germans believe it we do not know. Some, certainly, believe it wholeheartedly. Dorothy Thompson writes of such a case:

> "At Garmisch I met an American from Chicago. He had been at Oberammergau, at the Passion Play. 'These people are all crazy,' he said. 'This is not a revolution, it's a revival. They think Hitler is God. Believe it or not, a German woman sat next to me at the Passion Play and when the hoisted Jesus on the Cross, she said, 'There he is. That is our Fuehrer, our Hitler.' And when they paid out the thirty pieces of silver to Judas, she said 'That is Roehm, who betrayed the Leader.'" (568)

Extreme cases of this kind are probably not very numerous but it would be amazing if a small degree of the same type of thinking had not seeped into the picture of Hitler which many Germans hold.

Hitler
As His Associates Know Him

Part I

The picture the Nazi propaganda machine has painted of Hitler certainty seems like an extravagant one. Even if we ignore the deifying elements it seems like the fantasy of a superman - the paramount of all virtues. Extraordinary as it may seem, however, there are times at which he approximates such a personality and wins the respect and admiration of all his associates.

At such times he is a veritable demon for for work and often works for several days on end with little or no sleep. His powers of concentration are extraordinary and he is able to penetrate complex problems and reduce them to a few simple, fundamental factors. He prides himself on this talent and has said to various people:

> "I have the gift of reducing all problems to their simplest foundations ...A gift for tracing back all theories to their roots in reality."

And he really has it. Unencumbered with abstract theories or traditional points of view and prejudices he is able to look at complex problems in a rather naive way and pick out the most salient and significant elements and apply them to the present situation in a fairly simple and workable manner. To be sure, he never solves the entire problem in this way but only the human elements involved. Since this is the part which interests him most and produces immediate results, it has been rated very highly and has won the admiration of his close associates from the earliest days of his political career.

During these periods of activity Hitler is wholly consumed by the task confronting him. He has an amazing power of concentration. His judgements are quick and decisive. He is impatient to get things done and expects everyone to apply himself with an ardor equal to his own. He, therefore, demands great sacrifices from his associates.

At such times, however, he is also very human. He shows an unusual degree of considerateness towards them and a certain tolerance of their weaknesses. When he calls a halt for meals he will not eat until his entire staff has been served. When an overzealous servant insists on serving him before others he will often get up and take the plate over to one of his lowly assistants. During all of this he is in the best of spirit and jokes with everyone around him.

He has an extraordinary memory and continuously recalls amusing incidents from the past lives of those around him. These he tells to his staff at large. He is an excellent mimic and often plays out the roles of the individual involved to the great amusement of the staff while the individual must sit by and witness the performance much to his own embarassment. Nevertheless he is thoroughly flattered that the Fuehrer should single him out and remember in such detail. During these periods Hitler is also the soul of kindliness and generosity. He acts more like a big brother to his staff than as a Fuehrer and manages to endear himself to each and every one of them.

But, underneath, he is every inch the Fuehrer. He displays extraordinary courage and determination. He shows a great deal of initiative and is willing to assume full responsibility for the wisdom of the course he has mapped out. He is very persuasive and is able to muster and organize his people into an efficient smooth-running unit. Personal frictions disappear, for the time being, and everybody has a single thought in mind: To do what the Fuehrer wishes.

He works with great certainly and security and appears to have the situation entirely in hand. All kinds of facts and figures relevant to the problem flow from him without the slightest hesitation or effort, much to the amazement of those about him. He can cite the tonnages of ships in various navies:

> "He knows exactly what kind of armament, the kind of armor plates. the weight, the speed, and the number of the crew in every ship in the British navy. He knows the number of rotations of airplane motors in every model and type existant. he knows the number of shots a machine gun fires in a minute, whether it is a light, medium, or heavy one, whether it was made in the United States, Czecho-Slovakia or France."
> (Russell, 747)

Then, too, his staff has learned from past experience, that when Hitler is in one of these moods he approximates infallibility particularly when the support of the people is needed to carry through the project on which he is engaged. This may seem like an unwarranted statement but, if our study is to be complete, we must appraise his strengths as well as his weaknesses. It can scarcely be denied that he has some extraordinary abilities where the psychology of the average man is concerned. He has been able, in some manner or other, to unearth and apply successfully many factors pertaining to group psychology, the importance of which has not been generally recognized and some of which we might adopt to good advantage. These might be briefly summarized as follows:

(1) Full appreciation of the importance of the masses in the success of any movement. Hitler has phrased this rather well in MEIN KAMPF:

> "The lack of knowledge of the [unreadable] driving forces of [unreadable] led us to an insufficient evaluation of the importance of the great masses of the people; from this resulted the scant interest in the social position, the deficient courting [unreadable] soul of the nation's lower classes...." (p. 138)

(2) Recognition of the inestimable value of winning the support of youth; realization of the immense momentum given a social movement by the wild fervor and enthusiasm of young people as well as the importance of early training and indoctrination.

(3) Recognition of the role of women in advancing a new movement and of the fact that the reactions of the masses as a whole have many feminine characteristics. As early as 1923, he said to Hanfstaengl (902):

> "Do you know the audience at a circus is just like a woman (Die Masse, das Volk is wei ein Weib). Someone who does not understand the intrinsicly feminine character of the masses will never be an effective speaker. Ask yourself: 'What does a woman expect from a man?' Clearness,

decision, power and action. What we want is to get the masses to act. Like a woman, the masses fluctuate between extremes .... The crowd is not only like a woman, but women constitute the most important element in an audience. The women usualy lead, then follow the children and at last, when I have already won over the whole family - follow the fathers."

And in MEIN KAMPF, he writes:

"The people, in an overwhelming majority, are so feminine in their nature and attitude that their activities and thoughts are motivated less by sober consideration than by feeling and sentiment." (p.237)

(4) The ability to feel, identify with and express in passionate language the deepest needs and sentiments of the average German and present opportunities or possibilities for their gratification.

(5) Capacity to appeal to the most primitive, as well as the most ideal inclinations in man, to arouse the basest instincts and yet cloak them with nobility, justifying all actions as means to the attainment of an ideal goal. Hitler realized that men will not combine and dedicate the,selves to a common purpose unless this purpose be an ideal one capable of survival beyond their generation. He has also perceived that although men will die only for an ideal their continued zest and enterprise can be maintained only by a succession of more immediate and earthly satisfactions.

(6) Appreciation of the fact that the masses are as hungry for a sustaining ideology in political action as they are for daily bread. Any movement which does not satisfy this spiritual hunger in the masses will not mobilize their whole-hearted support and is destined to fail.

"All force which does not spring from a firm spiritual foundation will be hesitating and uncertain. It lacks the stability which can only rest on a fanatical view of life. (MK 222)

"Every attempt at fighting a view of life by means of force against it represents the form of an attack for the sake of a new spiritual direction. Only in the struggle of two views of life with each other can the weapon of brute force, used continuously and ruthlessly, bring about the decision in favor of the side it supports." (MK 223)

(7) The ability to portray conflicting human forces in vivid, concrete imagery that is understandable and moving to the ordinary man. This comes down to the use of metaphors in the form of imagery which, as Aristotle has said, is the most powerful force on earth.

(8) The faculty of drawing on the traditions of the people and by reference to the great classical mythological themes evoke the deepest unconscious emotions of the audience. The fact that the unconscious mind is more intensely affected by the great eternal symbols and themes is not generally understood by most modern speakers and writers.

(9) Realization that enthusiastic political action does not take place if the emotions are not deeply involved.

(10) Appreciation of the willingness, almost desire, of the masses to sacrifice themselves on the altar of social improvement or spiritual values.

(11) Realization of the importance of artistry and dramatic intensity in conducting large meetings, rallies and festivals. This involved not only an appreciation of what the artist - the writer, musician and painter - can accomplish in the way of evoking emotional responses but also the leader's recognition of the necessity of

his participation in the total dramatic effect as chief character and hero. Hitler has become master of all the arts of high-lighting his own role in the movement for a Greater Germany. Shirer (157) describes this very well:

"A searchlight plays upon his lone figure as he slowly walks through the hall, never looking to right or left, his right hard raised in salute, his left hand as the buckle of his belt. He never smiles - it is a religious rite, this procession of the moderm Messiah incarnate. Behind him are his adjutants and secret service men. But his figure alone is flooded with light.

"By the time Hitler has reached the rostrum, the masses have been so worked upon that they are ready to do his will...."

(12) A keen appreciation of the value of slogans, catchwords, dramatic phrases and [unreadable] epigrams in penetrating the deeper levels of the psyche. In speaking to Hanfstaengl on this point he once used the following figure of speech:

"There is only so much room in a brain, so much wall space, as it were, and if you furnish it with your slogans, the opposition has no place to put up any pictures later on, because the apartment of the brain is already crowded with your furniture." Hanfstaengl adds that Hitler has always admired the use the Catholic Church made of slogans and has tried to imitate it." (899)

(13) Realization of a fundamental loneliness and feeling of isolation in people living under modern conditions and a craving to "belong" to an active group which

carries a certain status, provides cohesiveness and gives the individual a feeling of personal worth and belongingness.

(14) Appreciation of the value underlying a hierarchical political organization which affords direct contact with each individual.

(15) Ability to surround himself with and maintain the allegiance of a group of devoted aides whose talents complement his own.

(16) Appreciation of winning confidence from the people by a show of efficiency within the organization and government. It is said that foods and supplies are already in the local warehouses when the announcement concerning the date of distribution is made. Although they could be distributed immediately the date is set for several weeks ahead in order to create an impression of super-efficiency and win the confidence of the people. Every effort is made to avoid making a promise which cannot be fulfilled at precisely the appointed time.

(17) Appreciation of the important role played by little things which affect the everyday life of the ordinary man in building up and maintaining the morale of the people.

(18) Full recognition of the fact that the overwhelming majority of the people want to be led and are ready and willing to submit if the leader can win their respect and confidence. Hitler has been very successful in this respect because he has been able to convince his followers of his own self-confidence and because he has guessed right on so many occasions that he has created the impression of infallibility.

(19) This was largely possible because he is so naturally a tactical genius. His timing of decisions and actions has almost been uncanny. As Thyssen puts it:

"Sometimes his intelligence is astonishing... miraculous political intuition, devoid of all moral sense, but extraordinarily precise. Even in a very complex situation he discerns what is possible and what is not."

(20) Hitler's strongest point is, perhaps, his firm belief in his mission and, in public, the complete dedication of his life to its fulfillment. It is the spectacle of a man whose convictions are so strong that he sacrifices himself for the cause which appeals to and is able to arouse similar convictions in others that induces them to follow his example. This demands a fanatical stubbornness which Hitler possesses to a high degree.

"Only a storm of glowing passion can turn the destinies of nations, but this passion can only be roused by a man who carries it within himself."

(21) He also has the ability to appeal to and arouse the sympathetic concern and protectiveness of his people, to represent himself as the bearer of their burdens and their future, with the result that he becomes a personal concern to individuals and many, particularly the women, feel tenderly and compassionately about him. They must always be careful not to inflict undue annoyance or suffering on the Fuehrer.

(22) Hitler's ability to repudiate his own conscience in arriving at political decisions has eliminated the force which usually checks and complicates the forward-going thoughts and resolutions of most socially responsible statesmen. He has, therefore, been able to take that course of action which appeals to him as most effective without pulling his punches. The result has been that he has frequently outwitted his adversaries and attained ends which would not have been as easily attained by a normal course. Nevertheless, it has helped to build up thte myth of his infallibility and invincibility.

(23) Equally important has been his ability to persuade others to repudiate their individual consciences and assume that role himself. He can then decree for the individual what is right and wrong, permissible or impermissible and can use them freely in the attainment of his own ends. As Goering has said: "I have no conscience. My conscience is Adolph Hitler."

(24) This has enabled Hitler to make full use of terror and mobilize the fears of the people which he evaluated with an almost uncanny precision.

(25) He has the capacity for learning from others even though he may be violently opposed to everything they believe and stand for. The use of terror, for example, he says he learned from the Communists, the use of slogans from the Catholic Church, the use of propaganda from the democracies, etc.

(26) He is a master of the art of propaganda. Ludecke writes:

> "He has a matchless instinct for taking advantage of every breeze to raise a political whirlwind. No official scandal was so petty that he could not magnify it into high treason; he could ferret out the most deviously [unreadable] corruption in high places and plaster the town with the bad news." (159)

His primary rules were: never allow the public to cool off; never admit a fault or wrong; never concede that there may be some good in your enemy; never leave room for alternatives; never accept blame; concentrate on one enemy at a time and blame him for everything that goes wrong; people will believe a big lie sooner than a little one; and if you repeat it frequently enough people will sooner or later believe it.

(27) He has the "never say die" spirit. After some of his severest set-backs he has been able to get his immediate

associates together and begin making plans for a "come-back". Events which would crush most individuals, at least temporarily, seem to act as stimulants to greater efforts in Hitler.

These are some of Hitler's outstanding talents and capacities. They have enabled him to attain a position of unprecedented power in an incredibly short perios of time, over a rarely used route. No other Nazi in a high position possesses these abilities in any comparable degree and consequently they could not displace him in the minds of the masses.

His associates recognize these capacities in Hitler and they admire and respect his extraordinary leadership qualities, particularly the influence he has over people. In addition they love him for his very human qualities when he is at his best and is engaged in some important undertaking. These are aspects of Hitler's personality we should never lose sight of when evaluating his hold on his associates or on the German people. He has a magnetic quality about him which, together with his past accomplishments, wins the allegiance of people and seems to rob them of their critical functions. It is a bond which does not easily dissolve even in the face of evidence that he is not always what he pretends to be - in fact is more often than not, the exact opposite.

We have reviewed Hitler's strength and briefly portrayed his character when he is at his best. It is now time to look at the other side of his personality - the side which is known only to those who are on fairly intimate terms with him.

Perhaps the truest words that Goebbels ever wrote are:

> "The Fuehrer does not change. He is the same
> now as he was when he was a boy" (387)

If we glance at his boyhood we find that Hitler was far from a model student. He studied what he wanted to study and did fairly well in these subjects. Things which did not interest him he simply ignored even though his marks were "unsatisfactory" or "failing". For over a year before his mother died, he did nothing, as far as can be determined, expect lie around the house or occasionally painting a few water-colors. Although they were in difficult financial circumstances he did not seek work or try to improve himself in school. He was self-willed, shy and inactive.

In Vienna, after his mother died, he continued this pattern even though he was frequently on the verge of starvation and reduced to begging on the streets. Hanisch, who was his flop-house buddy, reports that "he was never an ardent worker, was unable to get up in the morning, had difficulty in getting started and seemed to be suffering from a paralysis of the will." As soon as he had sold a picture and had a little money in his pocket he stopped work and spent time listening to parliament, reading newspapers in the cafes, or delivering lengthy political dissertations to his fellows in the hostel. This behavior he justified on the grounds that "he must have leisure, he was not a coolie." When Hanisch asked him one day what he was waiting for, Hitler replied: "I don't know myself."

As an adult he is still this little boy when he is not in one of his active moods. In 1931 Billing wrote:

> "Die inneren Schwierigkeiten einer Regierung Hitlers werden in der Person Hitler selbst liegen. Hitler wird nicht umhin koennen, sich an eine geregelte Geistige faetigkeit zu gowoehnen." (586)

Ludecke (168) also wrote:

> "He had a typical Austrian 'Schlamperei'. He suffered from an all-embracing disorderliness. Naturally this grew less in time but in the beginning it was apparent in everything."

It was indeed so apparent that early in the history of the movement the party engaged a secretary whose duty it was to keep track of Hitler and see to it that he fulfilled his duties and obligations. The move was only partially successful, however; "Hitler was always on the go but rarely on time" (Ludecke, 168). He is still rarely on time and frequently keeps important foreign diplomats, as well as his own staff, waiting for considerable periods of time.

Hitler
As His Associates Know Him

Part II

He is unable to maintain any kind of a working schedule. His hours are most irregular and he may go to bed any time between midnight and seven o'clock in the morning and get up anywhere from nine o'clock in the morning and two in the afternoon. In later years the hours tended to get later and it was unusual, just before the war, for him to go to bed before daybreak. The night, however, was not spent in working as his propaganda agents allege, but in viewing one or two feature movies, endless newsreels, listening to music, entertaining film stars or just sitting around chatting with his staff.

He seemed to have a violent dislike for going to bed or being alone. Frequently, he would ring for his adjutants in the middle of the night after his guests had gone home and demand that they sit up and talk to him. It was not that he had anything to say and often the adjutants would fall asleep listening to him talk about nothing of importance. As long as one of them remained awake, however, he would not be offended. There was an unwritten law among his immediate staff never to ask a question at these early morning sessions because to do so might get Hitler off on another subject and force them to remain for another hour.

Hitler sleeps very badly and has been in the habit for some years of taking a sleeping powder every night before retiring. It is possible that he demands someone to be with him in the hope that the powder will take effect and he will be overcome with sleep. His behavior, however, is not in keeping with this hypothesis for he carries on a monologue and frequently gets very much stirred up about the topic.

This is hardly conducive to sleep and we must suppose that there is some other reason for his late hours. Even after he has dismissed his adjutant and goes to bed he usually takes an armful of illustrated periodicals with him. These are usually magazines with pictures concerning naval and military matters and American magazines are usually included. Shirer (280) reports that he has been informed that since the war broke out Hitler has been keeping better hours and regularly has his first breakfast at seven A.M. and his second breakfast at nine A.M. This may have been so during the early days of the war but it is very doubtful that Hitler could keep up this schedule for any length of time.

Rauschning (275) claims that Hitler has a bed compulsion which demands that the bed be made in a particular way with the quilt folded according to a proscribed pattern and that a man must make the bed, before he can go to sleep. We have no other information on this subject but from his general psychological structure such a compulsion would be possible.

His working day before the war was equally disorderly. Rauschning reports, "he does not know how to work steadily. Indeed, he is incapable of working." He dislikes desk work and seldom glances at the piles of reports which are placed on his desk daily. No matter how important these may be or how much his adjutants may urge him to attend to the particular matter, he refuses to take them seriously unless it happens to be a project which interests him. On the whole, few reports interest him unless they deal with military or naval affairs or political matters. He seldom sits in a cabinet meeting because they bore him. On several occasions when sufficient pressure was brought to bear he did attend but got up abruptly during the session and left without apology. Later it was discovered that he had gone to his private theater and had the operator show some film that he particularly liked. On the whole, he prefers to discuss cabinet matters with each member in person and then communicate his decision to the group as a whole.

He has a passion for the latest news and for photographs of himself. If Hoffmann, the official Party photographer, happens to appear or someone happens to enter his office with a newspaper he will interrupt the most inportant meeting in order to scan through them Very frequently he becomes so absorbed in the news or in his own photographs that he completely forgets the topic under discussion. Ludecke (165) writes:

> "Even on ordinary days in those times, it was almost impossible to keep Hitler concentrated on one point. His quick mind would run away with the talk, or his attention would be distracted by the sudden discovery of the newspaper and he would stop to read it avidly, or he would interrupt your carefully prepared report with a long speech as though you were an audience...."

And Hanfstaengl reports that "his staff is usually in despair on account of his procrastination.... He never takes their protests in this respect very seriously and usually brushes them aside by saying, 'Problems are not solved by getting fidgety. If the time is ripe, the matter will be settled one way or another.'" (899)

Although Hitler tries to present himself as a very decisive individual who never hesitates when he is confronted by a difficult situation, he is usually far from it. It is at just these times that his procrastionation becomes most marked. At such times it is almost impossible to get him to take action on anything. He stays very much by himself and is frequently almost inaccessible to his immediate staff. He often becomes depressed, is in bad humor, talks little, and prefers to read a book, look at movies or play with architectural models. According to the Dutch report (656) his hesitation to act is not due to divergent views among his advisors. At such times, he seldom pays very much attention to them and prefers not to discuss the matter.

> "What is known as the mastery of material was quite unimportant to him. He quickly became impatient if the details of a problem were brought to him. He was greatly adverse to experts and had little regard for their opinion. He looked upon them as mere hacks, as brush-cleaners and color grinders...." (269)

On some occasions he has been known to leave Berlin without a word and go to Berchtesgaden where he spends his time walking in the country entirely by himself. Rauschning, who has met him on such occasions, says:

> "He recognizes nobody then. HE wants to be alone. There are times when he flees from human society." (275)

Roehm (176) frequently said, "Usually he solves suddenly, at the very last minute, a situation that has become intolerable and dangerous only because he vacillates and procrastinates."

It is during these periods of inactivity that Hitler is waiting for his "inner voice" to guide him. He does not think the problem through in a normal way but waits until the solution is presented to him. To Rauschning he said:

> "Unless I have the incorruptible conviction: THIS IS THE SOLUTION, I do nothing. Not even if the whole party tried to drive me to action.

I will not act; I will wait, no matter what
happens. But if the voice speaks, then I know
the time has come to act." (268)

These periods of indecision may last from a few days
to several weeks. If he is induced to talk about the
problem-solving this time he becomes ill-natured and
bad-tempered. However, when the solution has been given
to him he has a great desire to express himself. He then
calls in his adjutants and they must sit and listen to
him until he is finished no matter what time it happens
to be. On these occasions he does not want them to
question him or even to understand him. It seems that
he just wants to talk.

After this recital to his adjutants Hitler calls in his
advisers and informs them of his decision. When he has
finished they are free to express their opinions. If
Hitler thinks that one of these opinions is worthwhile
he will listen for a long time but usually these opinions
have little influence on his decision when this stage has
been reached. Only if someone succeeds in introducing
new factors is there any possibility of getting him to
change his mind. If someone voices the opinion that the
proposed plan is too difficult or onerous he becomes
extremely angry and frequently says:

"I do not look for people having clever ideas
of their own but rather people who are clever
in finding ways and means of carrying out my
ideas." (654)

As soon as he has the solution to a problem his mood
changes very radically. He is again the Fuehrer we have
described at the beginning of this section.

"He is very cheerful, jokes all the time and
does not give anybody an opportunity to speak,
while he himself makes fun of everybody."

This mood lasts throughout the period when necessary work

has been done. As soon as the requisite orders have bean given to put the plan into execution, however, Hitler seems to lose interest in it. He becomes perfectly calm, ocoupies himself with other matters and sleeps unusually long hours. (654)

This is a very fundamental trait in Hitler's character structure. He does not think things out in a logical and consistent fashion, gathering all available information pertinent to the problem, mapping out alternative courses of action and then weighing the evidence pro and con for each of them before reaching a decision. His mental processes operate in reverse. Instead of studying the problem as an intellectual would do he avoids it and occupies himself with other things until unconscious processes furnish him with a solution.

Having the solution he then begins to look for facts which will prove that it is correct. In this procedure he is very clever and by the time he presents it to his associates, it has the appearance of a rational judgment. Nevertheless, his thought processes proceed from the emotional to the factual instead of starting with the facts as an intellectual normally does. It is this characteristic of his thinking process which makes it difficult for ordinary people to understand Hitler or to predict his future actions. His orientation in this respect is that of an artist and not that of a statesman.

Although Hitler has been extremely successful in using this inspirational technique in determining his course of action (and we are reminded of his following his course with the precision of a sleep-walker) it is not without its shortcomings. He becomes dependent on his inner guide which makes for unpredictability on the one hand and rigidity on the other. The result is that he cannot modify his course in the face of unexpected developments or firm opposition. Strasser (297) tells us that:

"When he was then confronted by contradictory

facts he was left floundering."

And Roehm says that there is:

> "No system in the execution of his thoughts. He wants things his own way and gets mad when he strikes firm opposition on solid ground." (176)

This rigidity of mental functioning is obvious even in ordinary everyday interviews. When an unexpected question is asked, he is completely at a loss. Lochner (154) supplies us with an excellent description of this reaction:

> "I saw this seemingly super-self-confident man actually blush when I broached the subject of German-American relations.... This evidently caught him off-guard. He was not used to having his infallibility challenged. For a moment he blushed like a school-boy, hemmed and hawed, then stammered an embarrassed something about having so many problems to ponder that he had not yet had time to take up America."

Almost everyone who has written about Hitler has commented on his rages. These are well known to all of his associates and they have learned to fear them. The descriptions of his behavior during these rages vary considerably. The more extreme descriptions claim that at the climax he rolls on the floor and chews on the carpets. Shirer (279) reports that in 1938 he did this so often that his associates frequently referred to him as "Teppichfresser". Not one of our informants who has been close to Hitler, people like Hanfstaengl, Strasser, Rauschning, Hohenlohe, Friedelinde Wagner, and Ludecke, have ever seen him behave in this manner. Moreover they all are firmly convinced that this is a gross exaggeration and the informant of the Dutch Legation (655) says that this aspect must be relegated to the domain of "Greuelmaerchen."

Even without this added touch of chewing the carpet, his behavior is still extremely violent and shows an utter lack of emotional control. In the worst rages he undoubtedly acts like a spoiled child who cannot have his own way and bangs his fists on the tables and walls. He scolds and shouts and stammers and on some occasions foaming saliva gathers in the corners of his mouth. Rauschning, in describing one of these uncontrolled exhibitions, says:

> "He was an alarming sight, his hair disheveled, his eyes fixed, and his face distorted and purple. I feared that he would collapse or have a stroke." (110)

It must not be supposed, however, that these rages occur only when he is crossed on major issues. On the contrary, very insignificant matters might call out this reaction. In general they are brought on whenever anyone contradicts him, when there is unpleasant news for which he might feel responsible, when there is any skepticism concerning his judgment or when a situation arises in which his infallibility might be challenged or belittled. Von Weigand (492) reports that among his staff there is a tactic [spelling error of tactic in original] understanding:

> "For God's sake don't excite the Fuehrer - which means do not tell him bad news -- do not mention things which are not as he conceives them to be."

Voigt (591) says that:

> "Close collaborators for many years said that Hitler was always like this - that the slightest difficulty or obstacle could make him scream with rage...."

Many writers believe that these rages are just play acting. There is much to be said for this point of view since Hitler's first reaction to the unpleasant situation is not indignation, as one would ordinarily expect under these circumstances. He goes off into a rage or tirade without warning. Similarly, when he has finished, there is no aftermath. He immediately cools down and begins to talk about other matters in a perfectly calm tone of voice as though nothing had happened. Occasionally he will look around sheepishly, as if to see if anyone is laughing, and then proceeds with other matters, without the slightest trace of resentment.

Some of his closest associates have felt that he induces these rages consciously to frighten those about him. Rauschning (261), for example, says it is a:

"...technique by which he wouldthrow his entire entourage into confusion by well-timed fits of rags and thus make them more submissive."

Strasser (377) also believes this to be the case for he says:

"Rage and abuse became the favorite weapons in his armory."

This is not the time to enter into a detailed discussion concerning the nature and purpose of the rages. It is sufficient, for the present time, to realize that his associates are well aware that Hitler can and does behave in this way. It is a part of the Hitler they know and are forced to deal with. We may point out, however, that they are not conscious acting alone since it is quite impossible for an actor to actually become purple in the face unless he really is in an emotional state.

There are many other aspects of Hitler's personality, as it is known to his associates, which do not fit into the picture of the Fuehrer as it is presented to the German people. A few of the more important of these merit mention. Hitler is represented as a man of great courage, with nerves of steel who always is in complete control of every situation. Nevertheless, he often runs away from an unpleasant, unexpected or difficult situation.

Bayles (2) reports two incidents that illustrate this reaction:

> "Particularly noticeable is his inability to cope with unexpected situations, this having been amusingly revealed when he laid the cornerstone of the House of German Art in Munich. On this occasion he was handed a dainty, rococo hammer for delivering the three traditional strokes to the cornerstone, but not realizing the fragility of the rococo, he brought the hammer down with such force that at the very first stroke it broke into bits. Then, instead of waiting for another hammer, Hitler completely lost his composure, blushed, looked wildly about him in the manner of a small boy caught stealing jam, and almost ran from the scene leaving the cornerstone unlaid. His enjoyment of the Berlin Olympic Games was completely spoilt when a fanatical Dutch woman who had achieved a personal presentation suddenly clasped him in two hefty arms and tried to kiss him in plain view of 100,000 spectators. Hitler could not regain his composure or stand the irreverent guffaws of foreign visitors, and left the Stadium."

This type of behavior is illustrated even more clearly in relation to Gregor Strasser because the occasion was one of extreme importance to Hitler. Strasser threatened to split the Party if a definite program could not be agreed upon. Hitler avoided the situation as long as he possibly could in the hope that something might happen, that the situation would somehow solve itself. When it did not he agreed to Strasser's demand for a meeting in Leipzig at which their differences could be thrashed out. Strasser was in the restaurant at the appointed hour. Hitler came late. Hardly had he sat down to the table when he excused himself in order to go to the toilet. Strasser waited for some time and when Hitler did not return he began making inquiries. To his amazement he discovered that instead of going to the toilet Hitler had slipped out of the back door and driven back to Munich without discussing a single point. (378)

Heiden (527) also tells us that in 1923 he was in conference with Ludendorff when he suddenly rushed off without as much as an apology. In the spring of 1932 he ran out on a meeting of the Verband Bayrischer Industrieller before which he was to speak. This group was not kindly disposed to him but it was important for Hitler to win them over. He got up to speak:

> "..er stookt, sieht auf den Tisch, Schweigen alles sieht sich verblüefft an. Peinliche Minuten. Ploetzlich dreht sich Hitler auf dem Absatz um und geht ohne ein Wort an die Tuer."

The same thing happened a year later when, as Chancellor, he was to speak to the Reichsverband der Deutschen Presse, Again he sensed opposition in the group and again he fled from the scene, Olde (611) says:

> "Das ist ein Trick, den der Fuehrer noch oft anwerden wird: wenn die Situation peinlich wird, versteckt er sich."

At other times, when he finds himself in difficult situations, the great dictator who prides himself on his decisiveness, hardness and other leadership qualities, breaks down and weeps like a child appealing for sympathy. Raischning (267) writes:

> "In 1934 as in 1932 he complained of the ingratitude of the German people in the sobbing tones of a down-at-the-heel music-hall performer! A weakling who accused and sulked, appleaed and implored, and retired in wounded vanity ('If the German people don't want me!')

instead of acting."

Otto Strasser reports that on one occasion:

> "He seized my hands, as he had done two years before. His voice was choked with sobs, and tears flowed down his cheeks." (381)

Heiden (280) reporting a scene at which the Party leaders were waiting for the arrival of gregor Strasser:

> "'Never would I have believed it of Strasser,' he (Hitler) cried, and he laid his head on the table and sobbed. Tears came to the eyes of many of those present, as they saw their Fuehrer weeping. Julius Streicher, who had been snubbed by Strasser for years, called out from his humble place in the background: 'Shameful that Strasser should treat our Fuehrer like that!'"

In extremely difficult situations he had openly threatened to commit suicide. Sometimes it seems that he uses this as a form of blackmail while at other times the situation seems to be more than he can bear. During the Beer Hall Putsch he said to the officials he was holding as prisoners:

> "There are still five bullets in my pistol – four for the traitors, and one, if things go wrong, for myself," (253)

He also threatened to commit suicide before Mrs. Hanfstaengl directly after the failure of the Putsch, while he was hiding from the police in the Hanfstaengl home. Again in Landsberg he went on a hunger strike and threatened to martyr himself – an imitation of the Mayor of Cork. In 1930, he threatened to commit suicide after the strange murder of his niece, Geli, (302) of whom we shall speak later. In 1932, he again threatened to carry out this action if Strasser split the (98) Party.

In 1933 he threatened to do so if he was not appointed Chancellor (63), and in 1936, he promised to do so if the Occupation of the Rhineland failed. (255)

These, however, are relatively infrequent exhibitions although his associates have learned that they are always a possibility and that it is wise not to push the Fuehrer too far. More frequent are his depressions about which a great deal has been written. It is certain that he does have very deep depressions from time to time. During his years in Vienna (1907-1912), after his mother's death, he undoubtedly suffered from them a great deal. Hanisch reports (64):

> "I have never seen such helpless letting down in distress."

It is probably also true that he suffered from depressions during the war as Mend (199) reports.

After the death of his niece, Geli (1930), he also went into a severe depression which lasted for some time. Gregor Strasser actually feared that he might cnmmit suicide during this period and stayed with him for several days. There is some evidence (Strasser, 302) that he actually tried to do so and was prevented from carrying it out. It is also interesting to note that for several years after her death he went into a depression during the Christmas holidays and wandered around Germamy alone for days on end (957).

Rauschning gives us a vivid description of his condition after the Blood Purge of 1934. He writes (716):

> "Aber zunaechst machte auch er nioht den Eindruck des Siegers. Mit gedunsenen, verserrten Zuegen sass er mir gegenueber, als ich ihm Vortrag hielt. Seine Augen waren erloschen, er sah mich nicht an. Er spielte mit seien Fingern. Ich hatte nicht den Eindruck, dass er mir zuhoerte.... Waehrend der ganzen Zeit hatte ich den Eindruk,

dass Ekel, Ueberdruss und Verachtung in ihm herumstritten, und dass er mit seinen Gedanken ganz wo anders war.... Ich hatte gehoert, er sollte nur noch studenweis schlafen koennen... Nachts irrte er ruhelos umber. Schlafmittel halfen nicht.... Mit Weinkraempfen sollte er aus dem kurzem Schlaf aufwachen. Er haette sich wiederholt erbrochen. Mit Schuettelfrost habe er in Decken gehuellt im Seesel gesessen...Einmal wollte er alles erleuchtet und Menschen, viel Menschen um sich haben; im gleichen Augenblick haette er wieder neimanden sehen wollen...."

These are major crises in his life and we can assume that they probably represent his worst depressions. Undoubtedly he very frequently has minor ones when he withdraws from his associates and broods by himself, or periods when he refuses to see anyone and is irritable and impatient with those around him. On the whole, however, it appears that the reports of Hitler's depressions have been grossly exaggerated. Not one of our informants who has had close contact with him has any knowledge of his ever retiring to a sanatarium during such times and there is only one source which indicates that he ever sought psychiatric help and that was not accepted. We must assume that the many reports that have flourished in the newspapers have been plants by the Nazi Propaganda agencies to lure us into false expectations.

There are a number of other respects in which Hitler does not appear before his associates as the self-confident Fuehrer he likes to believe himself to be. One of the most marked of these is his behavior in the presence of accepted authority. Under these circumstances he is obviously nervous and very ill at ease. Many times he is downright submissive. As far back as 1923, Ludecke (166) reports that:

"In conference with Poehner, Hitler sat with his felt hat crushed shapeless in his hands. His mien was almost humble..."

Dissecting the Hitler Mind

Fromm (371) writes that at a dinner:

> "Hitler's eagerness to obtain the good graces of the princes present was subject to much comment. He bowed and clicked and all but knelt in his zeal to please oversized, ugly Princess Luise von Sachsen-Meiningen, her brother, hereditary Prince George, and their sister, Grand Duchess of Sachsen-Weimar. Beaming in his servile attitude he dashed personally to bring refreshments from the buffet."

On his visit to Rome, Hues (408) writes:

> "When leading Queen Helene in Rome he was like a fish out of water. He didn't know what to do with his hands."

To Hindenburg, he was extremely submissive. Pictures taken of their meetings illustrate his attitude very clearly. In some of them it looks almost as though he were about to kiss the President's hand. Flannery (698) also reports that when Hitler first met Petain he took him by the arm and escorted him to his car. Hanfstaengl (912) reports that he found Hitler outside the door of the banquet hall in which a dinner and reception were being given to the former Kaiser's wife. He was unable to bring himself to go in and meet her Highness alone. When Hanfstaengl finally persuaded Hitler to go in he was so ill at ease that he could only stammer a few words to Hermine and then excused himself. Many other examples could be cited. From the weight of evidence it seems certain that Hitler does lose his self-confidence badly when he is brought face to face with an accepted authority of high standing, particularly royalty.

This subservient attitude is also obvious in his use of titles. This is well described by Lania (148) reporting on Hitler's trial:

> "In the course of his peroration he came to speak

of Generals Ludendorff and von Seeckt; at such moments, he stood at attention and trumpeted forth the words 'General' and 'Excellency'. It made no difference that one of the generals was on his side, while the other, von Seeckt, Commander-in-Chief of the Reichswehr, was his enemy; he abandoned himself entirely to the pleasure of pronouncing the high-sounding titles. He never said 'General Seeckt', he said 'His Excellency Herr Colonel General von Seeeke, letting the words melt on his tongue and savoring their after-taste."

Many others have also commented on this tendency to use the full title. It also fits in with his very submissive behavior to his officers during the last war which has been commented upon by several of his comrades. It seems safe to assume that this is a fundamental trait in his character which becomes less obvious as he climbs the ladder but is present nevertheless.

The Fuehrer is also ill at ease in the company of diplomats and avoids contact with them as much as possible. Fromm (369) describes his behavior at a diplomatic dinner in the following words:

> "The Corporal seemed to be ill at ease, awkward and moody. His coat-tails embarrassed him. Again and again his hand fumbled for the encouraging support of his sword belt. Each time he missed the familiar cold bracing support, his uneasiness grew. He crumpled his handkerchief, tugged it, rolled it, just plain stage-fright."

Henderson (124) writes:

> "It will always be a matter of regret to me that I was never able to study Hitler in private life, as this might have given me the chance to see him under normal conditions and to talk with him as man to man. Except for a

few brief words at chance meetings, I never met him except upon official, and invariably disagreeable, business. He never attended informal parties at which diplomats might be present, and when friends of mine did try to arrange it, he always got out of meeting me in such a manner on the ground of precedent... But he always looked self-conscious when he had to entertain the diplomatic corps, which happened normally three times a year."

Hitler also becomes nervous and tends to lose his composure when he has to meet newspapermen. Being a genius of propaganda he realizes the power of the press in influencing public opinion and he always provides the press with choice seats at all ceremonies. When it comes to interviews, however, he feels himself on the defensive and insists that the questions be submitted in advance. When the interview takes place he is able to maintain considerable poise because he has his answers prepared. Even then he gives no opportunity to ask for further clarification because he immediately launches into a lengthy dissertation, which sometimes develops into a tirade. When this is finished, the interview is over (Oechsner, 665).

He is also terrified when he is called upon to speak to intellectuals (Wagner, 487) or any group in which he feels opposition or the possibility of criticism.

Hitler's adjustment to people in general is very poor. He is not really on intimate terms with any of his associates. Hess is the only associate, with the possible exception of Streicher, who has ever had the privilege of addressing him with the familiar "Du". Even Goering, Goebbels and Himmler must address him with the more formal "Sie" although each of them would undoubtedly be willing to sacrifice his right hand for the privilege of addressing him in the informal manner. It is true that outside of his official family there are a few people in Germany, notably Mrs. Bechstein and the Winifred Wagner family who address him as "Du" and call him by his nickname, "Wolf", but even these are few and far between. On the whole, he always maintains a considerable distance from other people. Ludecke, who was very close to him for a while, writes:

> "Even in his intimate and cozy moments, I sensed no attitude of familiarity towards him on the part of his staff; there was always a certain distance about him, that subtle quality of aloofness...."(180)

And Fry (577) says:

> "He lives in the midst of many men and yet he lives alone."

It is well-known that he cannot carry on a normal conversation or discussion with people. Even if only one person is present he must do all the talking. His manner of speech soon loses any conversational qualities it might have had and takes on all the characteristics of a lecture and may easily develop into a tirade. He simply forgets his companions and behaves as though he were addressing a multitude. Strasser (297) has given a good, brief description of his manner:

> "Now Hitler drew himself erect and by the far-away look in his eyes showed plainly that he was not speaking merely to me; he was addressing an imaginary audience that stretched far beyond the walls of the living room."

This is not only true in connection with political matters. Even when he is alone with his adjutants or immediate staff and tries to be friendly he is unable to enter into give-and-take conversation. At times he scans to want to get closer to people and relates personal experiences, such as, "When I was in Vienna," or "When I was in the Army,". But under these circumstances, too, he insists on doing all the talking and always repeats the same stories over and over again in exactly the same form, almost as though he had memorized them. The gist of most of these stories is contained in MEIN KAMPF. His friends have all heard them dozens of times but this does not deter him from repeating them again with great enthusiasm. Nothing but the most superficial aspects of these experiences are ever touched upon. It seems as though he is unable to give more of himself than that (Hanfstaengl, 898).

Price (230) says: "When more than two people are present, even though they are his intimate circle, there is no general discourse. Either Hitler talks and they listen, or else they talk among themselves and Hitler sits silent." And this is the way it seems to be. He is not at all annoyed when members of the group talk to each other unless of course he feels like doing the talking himself. But ordinarily he seem to enjoy listening to others while he makes believe that he is attending to something else. Nevertheless, he overhears everything which is being said and often uses it later on. (Hanfstaengl, 914) However, he does not give credit to the individual from whom he has learned it and simply gives it out as his own.

Rauschning (266) says:

> "He has always been a poseur. He remembers things that he has heard and has a faculty for repeating them in such a way that the listener is lead to believe that they are his own."

Roehm also complained of this:

> "If you try to tell him anything, he knows everything already. Though he often does what we advise, he laughs in our faces at the moment, and later does the very thing as if it were all his own idea and creation. He doesn't even seem to be aware of how dishonest he is." (176)

Another one of his tricks which drives people and particularly his associates to distraction is his capacity for forgetting. This trait has been commented upon so much that it scarcely needs mentioning here. We all know how he can say something one day and a few days later say the opposite, completely oblivious to his earlier statement. He does not only do this in connection with international affairs but also with his closest associates. When they show their dismay and call his attention to the inconsistency he flies off into a rage and demands to know if the other person thinks he is a liar. Evidently the other leading Nazis have also learned the trick, for Rauschning (266) says:

> "Most of the Nazis, with Hitler at their head, literally forget, like hysterical women, anything they have no desire to remember."

Although Hitler almost invariably introduces a few humorous elements into his speeches and gives the impression of considerable wit, he seems to lack any real sense of humor. He can never take a joke on himself. Heyst (600) says, "He is unable to purify his gloomy self with self-irony and humor." Von Wiegand (492) says he is extremely sensitive to ridicule and Huss says (408) "He takes himself seriously and will flare up in a tempermental rage at the least impingement by act or attitude on the dignity and holiness of state and Fuehrer." When everything is going well he sometimes gets into a gay and whimsical mood in a circle of close friends. His humor then is confined almost wholly to a kind of teasing or ribbing. The ribbing is usually in connection with alleged love affairs of his associates but are never vulgar and only hint at sexual factors (Hanfstaengl 910). Friedelinde Wagner provides us with an example of his teasing. Goering and Goebbels were both present at the time that he said to the Wagner family:

> "You all know what a volt is and an ampere, don't you? Right. But do you know what a

goebbels, a goering are? A goebbels is the amount of nonsense a man can speak in an hour and a goering is the amount of metal that can be pinned on a man's breast." (632)

His other form of humor is mimicking. Almost everyone concedes that he has great talent along these lines and he frequently mimics his associates in their presence much to the amusement of everyone except the victim. He also loved to mimic Sir Eric Phipps and later Chamberlain.

Hitler's poor adaptation to people is perhaps most obvious in his relations to women. Since he has become a political figure, his name has been linked with a great many women, particularly in the foreign press. Although the German public seem to know very little about this phase of his life, his associates have seen a great deal of it and the topic is always one for all kinds of conjectures. Roughly speaking, his relations to women fall into three categories; (a) much older women; (b) actresses and passing fancies, and (c) more or less enduring relationships.

A. As early as 1920 Frau Carola Hofman, a 61 year old widow, took him under her wing and for years played the part of [00010083.gif">[Page 77] foster mother. Then came Frau Helena Bechstein, the wife of the famous Berlin piano manufacturer, who took over the role. She spent large quantities of money on Hitler in the early days of the party, introduced him to her social circle and lavished maternal affection on hm, She often said that she wished that Hitler were her son and while he was imprisoned in Landsberg she claimed that she was his adopted mother in order that she fight visit him. Strasser (300) says that Hitler would often sit at her feet and lay his head against her bosom while she stroked his hair tenderly and murmured, "Mein Woelfchen".

Since he came to power things have not gone so smoothly. She seemed to find fault with everything he did and would scold him unmercifully, even in public. According to

Friedelinde Wagner (939) she is the one person in Germany who can carry on a monologue in Hitler's presence and who would actually tell him what she thought. During these violent'scoldings Hitler would stand there like an abashed schoolboy who had committed a misdemeanor. According to Hanfstaengl, Mrs. Bechstein had groomed Hitler in the expectation that he would marry her daughter, Lottie, who was far from attractive. Out of sense of obligation, Hitler did ask Lottie, but was refused, (904). Mrs. Bechstein was disconsolate over the failure of her plans and began to criticize Hitler's social reforms as well as his actions. Nevertheless, Hitler mde duty calls fairly regularly even though he postponed them as long as possible (939).

Then there was also Frau Victoria von Dirksen, who is alleged to have spent a fortune on him and his career (554), and a number of others. In more recent years, Mrs. Goebbels has taken over the role of foster-mother and looks after his comforts, supervises his household and bakes delicacies of which he is particularly fond. She, too, has been acting as a matchmaker in the hope that he might marry one of her friends and thereby draw the bond between them even tighter. To Ludecke, (177) she complained, "I am no good as a matchmaker. I would leave him alone with my most charming friesnds but he wouldn't respond." There was also his older half-sister, Angela, who kept house for him at Munich and Berchtesgaden and, for a time, seemed to play a mother's role.

Winifred Wagner, the daughter-in-law of Richard Wagner, has also caused a great deal of comment. She is English by birth, and, from all accounts, is very attractive and about Hitler's own age. She met Hitler in the early 1920's and since that time has been one of his staunch supporters. He became a frequent visitor at the Wagner home in Bayreuth and after his accession to power, built a house on the Wagner estate for himself and his staff. After the death. of Siegfried Wagner, reports all over the world had it that she would become Hitler's wife. But nothing happened in spite of the fact that it seemed like an ideal union from the point of view of both parties.

Nevertheless, Hitler continued to be a frequent guest at the Wagner's. It probably was the nearest thing to a home he has known since his own homebroke up in 1907. Mrs. Wagner undoubtedly did everything in her power to make him comfortable and Hitler felt very much at home. There were three small children, a boy and two girls (one of them is our informant, Friedelinde) which added considerably to the home atmosphere. The entire family called him by his nickname "Wolf" and addressed him as "Du". He felt so secure in this house that he often came and stayed without his bodyguard. He sometimes spent his Christmas holidays with the family and became very much a part of it. But further than that he was unwilling to go, even though the marriage would have been exceedingly popular with the German people.

B. Then there were a long line of 'passing fancies'. For the most part these were screen and stage stars. Hitler likes to be surrounded with pretty women and usually requests the moving picture companies to send over a number of actresses whenever there is a party in the Chancellory. He seems to get an extraordinary delight in fascinating these girls with stories about what he is going to do in the future or the same old stories about his past life. He also likes to impress them with his power by ordering the studios to provide them with better roles, or promising that he will see to it that they are starred in some forthcoming picture. Most of his associations with women of this type, and their number, is legion, does not go beyond this point as far as we have been able to discover. On the whole he seems, to feel more comfortable in the company of stage people than with any other group and often came down to the studio restaurants for lunch.

C. There have been several other women who have played a more or less important role in Hitler's life. The first of which we have any knowledge was Henny Hoffmann, the daughter of the official party photographer. Henny, according to reports, was little more than a prostitute and spent most of her time among the students in Munich, who alleged that she could be had for a few marks. Heinrich Hoffmann, her father, was a member of the Party and a closet friend of Hitler. By a queer twist of Fate, Hoffmann had taken a picture of the crowds in Munich at the outbreak of the last war. Later, when Hitler became prominent in Munich politics, Hoffmann discovered Hitler in the picture and called it to his attention. Hitler was delighted and a close relationship sprung up between them. Hoffmann' s wife was also very fond of Hitler and played a mother role towards him for a time.

With the death of Mrs. Hoffmann, the home went to pieces from a moral point of view and became a kind of meeting place for homosexuals of both sexes. There was a good deal of drinking and great freedom in sexual activities of all kinds. Hitler was frequently present at parties given in the Hoffmann home and became very friendly with Hermy. The relationship continued for some time until Henny, who was a very garrulous person by nature, got drunk one night and began to talk about her relationship to Hitler. Her father became enraged and for a time had little to do with Hitler.

Up to this time Hitler had steadfastly refused to have his photograph taken for publication on the grounds that it was better publicity to remain a mystery man and also because if his picture appeared it would be too easy to identify him when he crossed Communist territories. Shortly after the above described episode, Hitler named Hoffmann as the official Party photographer and gave him the exclusive right to his photographs. These privileges, so it is alleged, have, in the course of years netted Hoffmann millions of dollars. Among Hitler's associates, it was supposed that Hitler had committed some kind of sexual indiscretion with Henny and had bought Hoffmann's silence by granting him these exclusive rights.

In any event, Henny was soon married to Baldur von Schirach, the Leader of the Nazi Youth Movement who is reputed to be a homosexual. His family were violently opposed to the marriage but Hitler insisted. All differences between Hitler and Hoffmann seem to have disappeared and today he is one of Hitler's closest associates and exerts a great personal influence on the Fuehrer. We shall consider the nature of Hitler's indiscretion later in our study since it is not a matter of common knowledge and would lead us too far afield at the present time.

After the Henny Hoffmann episode, Hitler began to appear in public with his niece, Geli, the daughter of his half-sister, Angela, who had come to keep house for Hitler in 1924. At the time this relationship matured her mother had gone to Berchtesgaden and Hitler and Geli were living alone in his Munich flat. They became inseparable companions and became the subject of much comment in Party circles. Many of the members, particularly Gregor Strasser, felt that this was poor publicity and was creating a good deal of unfavorable talk. Other members had Hitler brought on the carpet to explain where he was getting the money to clothe Geli and sport her around if he was not using Party funds for this purpose.

Hitler became very jealous of Geli's attention and refused to let her go out with any other men. Some claim that he kept her locked in during the day when he could not take her with him. For several years the relationship continued over the opposition of the Party. Then one day Geli was found dead in Hitler's apartment - she had died from a bullet fired from Hitler's revolver. There was considerable commotion. The coroner's verdict was suicide but Geli was buried in hallowed ground by a Catholic clergy. There was much speculation whether she killed herself or was killed by Hitler. Whatever the facts my be, Hitler went into a profound depression which lasted for months. During the first days after the funeral, Gregor Strasser remained with him in order to prevent him from committing suicide. Ludecke (178) says: "The special quality of Hitler's affection (for Geli) is still a mystery to those closest to him."

For a few years after Geli's death, Hitler had little to do with women except in a very superficial way. Along about 1932, however, he became interested in Eva Braun, Hoffmann's photographic. assistant. This relationship did not develop very rapidly but it has contimed. In the course of time, Hitler has bought her many things including high-powered automobiles and a house between Munich and Berchtesgaden where, it is alleged, he frequently spends the night on the way to or from his country estate. Eva Braun is also frequently a guest at Berchtesgaden and in Berlin.

Oechsner was told that after one of her visits in Berchtesgaden some of her underwear was found in Hitler's bedroom. Wiedemann, according to Hohenlohe, says that she has sometimes spent the entire night in Hitler's bedroom in Berlin. It is reported by Norburt (605) that Eva moved into the Chancellory on December 16, 1939 and it is said that Hitler intends to marry her when the war is over. Beyond that, we know nothing about this affair except that Eva Braun has twice tried to commit suicide and that one of Hitler's bodyguards hurled himself from the Kehlstein because he was in love with her but could not respass [error in original document] the Fuehrer's domain.

The affair with Eva Braun was not exclusive, however. During this period he has also seen a good deal of at least two moving picture actresses. These have been more enduring than most of his associations with actresses and much more intimate. Both of these girls were frequently invited alone to the Chancellory late at night and departed in the early hours of the morning. During their stay they were alone with Hitler behind closed doors so that not even his immediate staff knows what transpired between them. The first of these relationships was with Renarte Mueller who connitted suicide by throwing herself from the window of a Berlin hotel. The other was with Leni Riefenstahl who continued to be a guest at the Chancellor up to the outbreak of the war.

Hitler's associates know that in respect to women Hitler is far from the ascetic he and the Propaganda Bureau would like to have the German public believe. None of them with the possible exception of Hoffmann and Schaub (his personal adjutant), know the nature of his sexual activities. This has led to a great deal of conjecture in Party circles. There are some who believe that his sex life is perfectly normal but restricted. Others, that he is immune from such temptations and that nothing happens when he is alone with girls. Still others believe that he is homosexual.

The latter belief is based largely on the fact that during the early days of the Party many of the inner circle were well-known homosexuals. Roehm made no attempt to hide his homosexual activities and Hess was generally known as "Fraulein Anna". There were also many others, particularly in the early days of the movement, and it was supposed, for this reason, that Hitler, too, belonged to this category.

In view of Hitler's pretense at purity and the importance of his mission for building a Greater Germany, it is extraordinary that he should be so careless about his associates. He has never restricted them in any way except at the time of the Blood Purge in 1934 when his excuse was that he had to purge the party of these undesirable elements. At all other times, he has been liberal to a fault. Lochner reports:

> "The only criterion for membership in the Party was that the applicant be 'Unconditionally obedient and faithfully devoted to me'. When someone asked if that applied to thieves and

criminals, Hitler said, 'Their private lives don't concern me.' "

Ludecke (179) claims that in speaking of some of the moralists who were complaining about the actions of his S.A. men, Hitler said:

"He would rather his S.A.men took the women than some fat-bellied moneybag. 'Why should I concern myself with the private lives of my followers ... apart from Roehm's achievements, I know that I can absolutely depend on him.' "

Rauschning says (264) that the general attitude in the Party was: "Do anything you like but don't get caught at it."

This attitude towards his associates certainly did not make for high standards in the Party. Capt. von Mueke resigned from the Party on the grounds that:

"Die Voelkische partei ist nicht mehr die Partei der anstaendigen Leute, sie ist herunter gekommon und korrupt. Kurz, das ist ein Saustall"(614)

Rauschning (276) expresses a similar sentiment:

"Most loathsome of all is the reeking miasma of furtive, unnatural sexuality that fills and fouls the whole atmosphere around him, like an evil emanation. Nother [error in original document] in this environment is straightforward. Surreptitious relationships, substitutes and symbols, false sentiments and secret lusts - nothing in this man's surroundings is natural and genuine, nothing has the openness of a natural instinct."

One of Hitler's reactions which is carefully hidden from the public is his love for pornography. He can scarcely wait for the next edition of DER STUERMER to appear and when it reaches him he goes through it avidly. He seems to get great pleasure out the dirty stories and the cartoons that feature this sheet. (658: 261). To Rauschning Hitler said that the STUERMER "was a form of pornography permitted in the Third Reich". In addition, Hitler has a large collection of nudes and, according to Hanfstaengl and others, he also enjoys viewing lewd movies in his private theatre, some of which are prepared by Hoffmann for his benefit.

He also likes to present himself as a great authority and lover of good music. One of his favorite pastimes is to lecture on Wagner and the beauty of his operatic music. There can be no doubt concerning his enjoyment of Wagnerian music and that he gets considerable inspiration from it. Oechsner (675) reports that he has been able to observe Hitler closely while he was listening to music and saw, "grimaces of pain and pleasure contort his face, his brows knit, his eyes close, his mouth contact tightly." Hitler has said, "For me, Wagner is something godly, and his music is my religion. I go to his concerts as others go to church."

According to Hanfstaengl, however, he is not a lover of good music in general (895). He says that about 85% of Hitler's preferences in music are the normal program music in Vienna cafes. This is probably why Hitler rarely attends concerts and in later years, seldom goes to the opera. His preferences now seem to run to musical comedies and cabarets in addition to the movies he sees at the Chancellory. Pope (229) says that Hitler frequently visited the MERRY WIDOW in which an American actress played the lead. He says, "I have seen Hitler nudge his gauleiter, Wagner, and smirk when Dorothy does her famous backbending number in the spotlight." In this number, Dorothy's costume consists of a pair of transparent butterfly wings, or sometimes nothing at all. Hitler watches the performance through opera glasses and sometimes has command performances for his private benefit.

Much has been written by the Nazi propaganda bureau about his modest way of living. This, through the eyes of his associates, has also been vastly overrated. Although he is a vegetarian, most of them feel that his meals are scarcely to be considered as a form of deprivation. He eats large quantities of eggs prepared in 101 different ways by the best chef in Germany and there are always quantities and a large variety of fresh vegetables prepared in unusual ways. In addition. Hitler consumes incredible quantities of pastries and often as much as two pounds of chocolates in the course of a single day. Nor are his personal tastes particularly inexpensive. Although his clothes are simple, he has an incredible number of each article of clothing. All are made of the finest materials that can be procured and made up by the best workmen.

He also has a passion for collecting paintings and when he has his heart set on one, the sky is the limit is far as price is concerned. The only thing that is really modest about his living arrangements is his bedroom which is extremely simple and contains only a metal bed (decorated with ribbons at the head), a painted chest of drawers and a few straight chairs. Friedelinde Wagner and Hanfstaengl, both of whom have seen the room with their own eyes, have described it in identical terms: namely that it is a room that one would expect a maid to have and not a Chancellor.

Although he is presented to the German public as a man of extraordinary courage, his immediate associates frequently have occasion to question this. Several occasions have been reported on which he has not carried through his own program because he feared opposition. This is particularly true in connection with his Gauleiters. He seems to have a particular fear of these people and rather than meet opposition from them, he usually tries to find out on which side of an issue the majority have aligned themselves before he meets with them. When the meeting takes place, he proposes a plan or course of action which will fit in with the sentiments of the majority. (718)

According to Hohenlohe he also backed down before three Army generals when they protested against the rapid developments in the Danzig question, and that before Munich, he decided to postpone the war because he discovered that the crowds watching the troops marching under the Chancellory windows were unenthusiactic (661).

Furthermore, they must wonder about the necessity of the extreme precautions that are taken for his safety. Most of these are carefully concealed from the German public. When Hitler appears he looks for all the world like an extremely brave man as he stands up in the front seat of his open car and salutes. The people do not inow of the tremendous number of secret service men who constantly mingle with the crowds in addition to the guards who line the streets through which he is to pass. Neither do they know of all the precautions taken at the Chancellory or at Berchtesgaden.

Before the war his house at Berchtesgaden was surrounded with eight miles of electrified wire. Pillboxes and anti-aircraft batteries were set up in the surrounding hills (Morrell, 462). When he visited at Bayreuth, troops were sent in weeks in advance to set up machine-gun nests and anti-aircraft batteries in the hills immediately adjoining (Wagner, 934). Lochner (158) reports that when he travels in a special train he is accompanied by 200 SS guards who are more heavily armed than the retinue of any German emperor. After the war started, his train was heavily armored and equipped with anti-aircraft fore and aft. And, yet, when the newsreels show him at the front, he is the only one who does not wear a steel helmet.

There is, consequently, a considerable discrepancy between Hitler as he is known to the German. people and Hitler as he is known to his associates. Nevertheless, it appears that most of his associates have a deep allegience to Hitler personally and are quite ready to forgive or ignore his shortcomings. In many cases, it seems as though his asociates are quite oblivious to the contradictory traits in his character - to them he is still the Fuehrer and they live for the moments when he actually plays this role.

Hitler
As He Knows Himself

Part I

Hitler has always been extremely secretive in all his dealings. Hanfstangl tells us that this trait is carried to such a degree that he never tells one of his immediate associates what he has been talking about or arranged with another. His mind is full of compartments, Hanfstangl says, and his dealings with every individual are carefully pigeon-holed. What has been filed in one pigeon-hole is never permitted to mix with that in another. Everything is scrupulously kept locked up in his mind and is only opened when he needs the material.

This is also true of himself. We have already seen how he has steadfastly refused to divulge anything about his past to his associates. This, he believed, was something which did not concern them in any way and consequently he has kept the pigeonhole tightly closed. He talks almost continually about everything under the sun - except himself. What really goes on in his mind is almost as great a mystery as his past life.

Nevertheless, it would be helpful, and interesting to open this pigeon-hole and examine its contents. Fortunately, a few fragments of information concerning his past life have been unearthed in the course of time and these are extremely valuable as a background for understanding his present behavior., Then, too, we have records of attitudes and sentiments expressed in speeches and writings. Although these utterances are confined to a rather limited area, they do represent the products of some of his mental processes and consequently give us some clue to what goes on behind those much discussed eyes, of which Rauschning writes:

> "Anyone who has seen this man face to face, has met his uncertain glance, without depth or warmth, from eyes that seem hard and remote, and has then seen that gaze grow rigid, will certainly have experienced the uncanny feeling: 'That man is not normal.'"

In addition, we have descriptions of his overt behavior in the face of varied circumstances. We must assume that these, too, are the products of his psychological processes and that they reflect what is going on behind the scenes. All of this, however, would be insufficient data for an adequate picture of Hitler, as he knows himself, in everyday life. Fortunately, patients with behavior patterns, tendencies and sentiments very similar to those that Hitler has expressed are not unknown in psychoanalytical practice. From our knowledge of what goes on in the minds of these patients, together with a knowledge of their past histories, it may be possible to fill in some of the gaps and make some deductions concerning his extraordinary mode of adjustment.

We have learned from the study of many cases that the present character of an individual is the product of an evolutionary process, the beginnings of which are to be found in infancy. The very earliest experiences in the lifetime of the individual form the foundation upon which the character is gradually structured as the individual passes through successive stages of development and is exposed to the demands ant influences of the world around him. If this is true, it would be well for us to review briefly Hitler's past history, as far as it is known, in the hope that it may cast some light upon his present behavior and the course he is most likely to pursue in the future. Such a review of his past is also pertinent to our study insofar as it forms the background through which Hitler sees himself. It is a part of him he must live with, whether he likes it or not.

There is a great deal of confusion in studying Hitler's family tree. Much of this is due to the fact that the name has been spelled in various ways: Hitler, Hidler, Hiedler and Huettler. It seems reasonable to suppose, however, that it is fundamentally the same name spelled in various ways by different members of what was basically an illiterate peasant family. Adolph Hitler himself signed his name Hittler on the first party membership blanks, and his sister at the present time spells her name Hiedler. Another element of confusion is introduced by the fact that Adolph's mother's mother was also named Hitler which later became the family name of his father. Some of this confusion is dissipated, however, when we realize that Adolph' s parents had a common ancestor (father's grandfather and mother's great-grandfather), an inhabitant of the culturally bakcward [error in original document] Waldviertel district of Austria.

Adolph's father, Alois Hitler, was the illegitimate son of Maria Anna Schicklgruber. It is generally supposed that the father of Alois Hitler was a Johann Georg Hiedler, a miller's assistant. Alois, however, was not legitimized, and bore his mother's name until he was forty years of age when he changed it to Hitler. Just why this was done is not clear, but it is generally said among the villagers that it was necessary in order to obtain a legacy. Where the legacy came from is unknown. One could suppose that Johann Georg Hiedler relented on his deathbed and left an inheritance to his illegitimate son together with his name. However, it is not clear why he did not legitimise the son when he fineally married the mother thirty-five years earlier. Why the son chose to take the name Hitler instead of Hiedler, if this is the case, is a mystery which remains unsolved. Unfortunately, the date of the death of Hiedler has not been established and consequently we are unable to relate these two events in time. A peculiar series of events prior to Hitler's birth leaves plenty of room for speculation.

There are some people who seriously doubt that Johann

Georg Hiedler was the father of Alois. Thyssen and Koehler, for example, claim that Chancellor Dollfuss had ordered the Austrian police to conduct a thorough investigation into the Hitler family. As a result of this investigation a secret document was prepared which proved that Maria Anna Schicklgruber was living in Vienna at the time she conceived. At that time she was employed as a servant in the home of Baron Rothschild. As soon as the family discovered her pregnancy she was sent back to her home in Spital where Alois was born. If it is true that one of the Rothschilds is the real father of Alois Hitler, it would make Adolph a quarter Jew. According to these sources, Adolph Hitler knew of the existence of this document and the incriminating evidence it contained. In order to obtain it he precipitated events in Austria and initiated the assassination of Dollfuss. According to this story, he failed to obtain the document at that time, since Dollfuss had secreted it and, had told Schuschnigg of its whereabouts so that in the event of his death the independence of Austria would remain assured. Several stories of this general character are in circulation.

Those who lend credence to this story point out several factors which seem to favor its plausibility:

(a) That it is unlikely that the miller's assistant in a small village in this district would have very much to leave in the form of a legacy.

(b) That it is strange that Johann Hiedler should not claim the boy until thirty-five years after he had married the mother and the mother had died.

(c) That if the legacy were left by Hiedler on the condition that Alois take his name, it would not have been possible for him to change it to Hitler.

(d) That the intelligence and behavior of Alois, as well as that of his two sons, is completely out of keeping with that usually found in Austrian peasant families.

They point out that their ambitiousness and extraordinary political intuition is much more in harmony with the Rothschild tradition.

(e) That Alois Schicklgruber left his home village at an early age to seek his fortune in Vienna where his mother had worked

(f) That it would be peculiar for Alois Hitler, while working as a customs official in Braunau, should choose a Jew named Prinz, of Vienna, to act as Adolph's godfather unless he felt some kinship with the Jews himself.

This is certainly a very intriguing hypothesis and much of Adolph's later behavior could be explained in rather easy terms on this basis. However, it is not absolutely necessary to assume that he had Jewish blood in his veins in order to make a comprehensive picture of his character with its manifold traits and sentiments. From a purely scientific point of view, therefore, it is sounder not to base our reconstruction on such slim evidence but to seek firmer foundations. Nevertheless, we can leave it as a possibility which requires further verification.

In any event, Maria Ann Schicklgruber died when he was five years of age. When he was thirteen he left the Waldviertel and went to Vienna where he learned to be a cobbler. The next twenty-three years of his life are largely unaccounted for. It seems probable that during this time he joined the army and had perhaps been advanced to the rank of non-commissioned officer. His service in the army may have helped him to enter the Civil Service as Zellamtsoffizial later on.

His married life was stormy. His first wife (born Glasl-Hoerer) was about thirteen years older than himself. She is alleged to have been the daughter of one of his superiors and seems to have been in poor health. In any event, the marriage turned out badly and they finally separated since, as Catholics a complete divorce was not possible. His first wife died in 1883.

In January, 1882, Franziska Matzelsberger gave birth to an illegitimate son who was named Alois. After the death of his first wife on April 6, 1883, Alois Hitler married Franziska Matzelsberger on May 22, 1888 and legitimized his son,. On July 28, 1883 his second wife bore him another child, Angela, and a year later, on August 10, 1884, she also died. During the time of his first marriage the couple had taken as a foster-daughter Klara Poelzl, Alois Hitler's second cousin, once removed. He had reared her up to the time of the separation from his first wife when she went to Vienna as a servant. During the last months of the life of his second wife, Klara Poelzl returned to his home to look after the invalid and the two children. She remained in his home as housekeeper after the death of his second wife and on January 7, 1885 he married her.

On May 17, 1885 she gave birth to a son who died in infancy. It is alleged by William Patrick Hitler that an illegitimate child was born previously, but we have no other record of this. In any event, at least one child was conceived out of wedlock. Four more children were born of this union. This is certainly a tempestuous married life for a customs officer - three wives, seven or possibly eight children, one divorce, at least one birth and possibly two before marriage, two directly after the wedding, one wife thirteen years older than himself and another twenty-three years younger, one the daughter of a superior, one a waitress, and the third a servant and his foster-daughter. All of this, of course, has never been mentioned by Hitler. In MEIN KAMPF he gives a very simple picture-of conditions in his father's home.

Very little is known about Alois Hitler's character. It seems that he was very proud of his achievements in the Civil Service and yet he retired from this service at the astonishing age of fifty-six, four years after Adolph was born. In very rapid succession the family moved into several different villages and the father tried his hand at farming. It is said, however, that he always wore his customs official's uniform and insisted on being addressed as Herr Oberoffizial Hitler. According to reports, he liked to lord it over his neighbors whom he may have looked down upon as "mere" peasants. In any event, it seems quite certain that he enjoyed sitting in the tavern and relating his adventures as a customs official and also in discussing political topics.

He died on his way to the tavern in Leonding from a stroke of apoplexy in 1903.

He is generally described as a very domineering individual who was a veritable tyrant in his home. William Patrick Hitler says that he has heard from his father, Adolph's elder half-brother, that he used to best the children unmercifully. On one occasion it is alleged he beat the older son into a state of unconsciousness and on another occasion beat Adolph so severely that he left him for dead. It is also alleged that he was somewhat of a drunkard and that frequently the children would have to bring him home from the taverns. When he reached home a grand scene would take place during which he would beat wife, children and dog rather indiscriminately. This story is generally accepted and yet there is little real evidence in favor of it except what Hitler himself tells us in MEIN KAMPF.

Heidan, who interviewed a number of the villagers in places where the family lived, had nothing of this sort to report. They found the old man rather amusing and claimed that his home life was very happy and quiet except when his wife's sister came to visit with the family. Why this should be a disturbing factor is unknown. Heiden suspects that the legacy was a bone of contention.

There is some doubt about the complexion of Alois Hitler's political sentiments. Hanisch reports "Hitler heard from his father only praise of Germany and all the faults of

Austria." According to Heiden, more reliable informants claim that the father, though full of complaints and criticisms of the government he served, was by no means a German nationalist. They say he favored Austria against Germany and this coincides with William Patrick Hitler's information that his grandfather was definitely anti-German just as his own father was.

Mother Klara Poelzl, as has been said, was the foster-daughter of her husband and twenty-three years his junior. She came from old peasant stock, was hard-working, energetic and conscientious. Whether it was due to her years of domestic service or to her upbringing, her home was always spotlessly clean, everything had its place and not a speck of dust was to be found on the furniture. She was very devoted to her children and, according to William Patrick Hitler, a typical step-mother to her step-children. According to Dr. Bloch who treated her, she was a very sweet and affectionate woman whose life centered around her children and particularly Adolph, who was her pet. She spoke very highly of her husband and his character and the happy life they had together. She felt it was a real deprivation for the children to have lost their father while they were still so young.

One could question her background. Her sister is married and has two sons, one of whom is a hunchback and has an impediment in his speech. When we consider that Klara Poelzl may have lost one child before her marriage to Alois Hitler, another son born in 1885 who died in 1887, another son born in 1894 who died in 1900, and a girl who was born in 1886 and died in 1888, one has grounds to question the purity of the blood. There is even cause for greater suspicion when we learn from Dr. Bloch that he is certain that there was a daughter, slightly older than Adolph, who was an imbecile. He is absolutely certain of this because he noticed at the time that the family always tried to hide the child and keep her out of the way when he came to attend the mother. It is possible that this is Ida who was born in

1886 and who is alleged to have died in 1888, except that Dr. Bloch believes that this girl's name was Klara. He may, however, be mistaken in this particularly since both names end in "a" and he never had any close contact with her. There is no other record of a Klara anywhere in the records.

The younger sister, Paula, is also said to be a little on the stupid side, perhaps a high-grade moron. This is certainly a poor record and one is justified in suspecting some constitutional weakness. A syphilitic taint is not beyond the realm of possibility. The mother died following an operation for cancer of the breast on December 21,1907. All biographers have given the date of her death as December 21, 1906 but Dr. Bloch's records show clearly that she died in 1907 and John Gunther's record of the inscription on her tombstone corroborates this. The last six months of her life were spent in extreme pain and during the last week it was necessary to give her injections of morphine daily.

It is often alleged that she was of Czech origin and spoke only a broken German and that consequently Adolph may have been ashamed of her among his playmates. This is almost certainly untrue. Dr. Bloch reports that she did not have any trace of an accent of any kind nor did she show any Czech characteristics. Alois Hitler's first wife was of Czech origin and later writers may have confused her with Adolph's mother.

Siblings

Alois, Jr

Alois Hitler, Jr. was born January 13, 1882, the illegitimate son of the father's second wife born during the lifetime of the first wife. He is the father of William Patrick Hitler, one of our informants. He seems to have taken very much after his father in some respects. He left the parental home before the death of his father because, according to his son, he could tolerate it no longer. His step-mother, according to the story, made life very difficult for him and continually antagonized her husband against him. It seems that Alois, Jr. had considerable talent for mechanical pursuits and his father had planned on sending him to a technical school for training as an engineer. Until his third marriage the father was very fond of his oldest boy and all his ambitions were wrapped up in him. But the step-mother systematically undermined this relationship and finally persuaded the father that Alois, Jr. was unworthy and that he should save his money for the education of her son, Adolph. She was finally successful and Alois, Jr. was sent away from home as an apprentice waiter.

Evidently the profession of waiter did not intrigue him, for in 1900 he received a five-months' sentence for thievery and in 1902 he was sentenced to eight months in jail for the same reason. He then went to London where he obtained a position as a waiter and, in 1909, married Bridget Dowling, an Irish girl. In 1911 William Patrick Hitler was born and in 1915 his father deserted the family and returned to Germany. The family was not a happy one and broke up several times in the course of these four years. It is alleged that the father drinks quite frequently and would then come home and create tremendous scenes during which he frequently beat his wife and tried to beat the small infant. During these four years when his mother and father had separated for a time, his father did go to Vienna. This would agree with Hanfstangl's conviction that Alois, Jr. was in Vienna at the same time that Adolph was there.

In 1924 Alois, Jr. was brought before the court of Hamburg charged with bigamy. He was sentenced to six months in prison but since his first wife did not prosecute the sentence was suspended. He has an illegitimate child by the second wife who lives in Germany. During all these years he has never sent any money for the support of his first wife or child. Up until the time of the inflation it is alleged that he had a very successful business in Germany. The business failed and he has had various jobs up until 1934 when he opened a restaurant in Berlin which became a popular meeting-place for S.A. men.

According to the son, Alois, Jr. heartily disliked Adolph as a boy. He always felt that Adolph was spoiled by his mother and that he was forced to do many of the chores that Adolph should have done. Furthermore, it seems that Adolph occasionally got into mischief which his mother would blame on Alois and Alois would have to take the punishment from his father. He used to say as a boy he would have liked to have wrung Adolph's neck on more than one occasion and considering the circumstances this is probably not far from the truth. Since Hitler came to power, the two brothers have practically no contact with each other. They have come together a few times but the meeting is usually unpleasant, with Adolph taking a very high-handed attitude and laying down the law to the rest of the family. Alois, Jr. is not mentioned in MEIN KAMPF and only a few people in Germany know of his relationship to Hitler.

William Patrick Hitler

He is a young man of thirty-two, the son of Alois, Jr., who has not amounted to much. Before his uncle came to power he worked as a bookkeeper in London. When his uncle became famous he obviously expected that something would be done for his family. He gave up his job in London and went to Germany where he had some contact with Adolph Hitler. The latter, however, was chiefly interested in keeping him under cover and provided him with a minor job in the Opal Automobile Company. It is my impression that William Patrick was quite ready to blackmail both his father and his uncle but that things did not work out as planned. He returned to England and, as a British subject, came to this country where he is a professional speaker. He is also engaged in writing a book about his associations and experiences in Hitler Germany.

Angela

She is an elder half-sister of Adolph. She seems to be
the most normal one in the family and from all reports
is rather a decent and industrious person. During her
childhood she became very fond of Adolph despite the fact
that she had the feeling that his mother was spoiling
him. She is the only one of the family with whom Adolph
has had any contact in later years and the only living
relative Hitler ever mentioned. When his mother died in
1907 there was a small inheritance which was to be divided
among the children. Since the two girls had no immediate
means of earning a livelihood the brothers turned over
their share to help the girls along. Adolph turned his
share over to Angela while Alois turned his over to a
younger sister, Paula. Angela later married an official
named Raubal in Linz who died not long afterwards. She
then went to Vienna where, after the war, she was manager
of the Mensa Academica Judaica. Some of our informants
knew her during this time and report that in the student
riots Angela defended the Jewish students from attack,
and on several occasions beat the Aryan students off the
steps of the dining hall with a club. She is a rather
large, strong peasant type of person who is well able to
take an active part.

After Adolph was discharged from the army at the close
of the last war, it is alleged that he went to Vienna
and visited Angela with whom he had had no contact
for ten years. While he was confined in Landsberg she
made the trip from Vienna to visit him. In 1924 she
moved to Munich with her daughter, Geli, and kept
house for Adolph. Later, she took over the management
of Berchtesgaden. In 1936 friction developed between
Adolph and Angela and she left Berchtesgaden and moved
to Dresden where she married Professor Hamitsch. It is
reported by William Patrick that the cause of the break
was the discovery by Hitler that she was in a conspiracy
with Goering to purchase the land adjoining Hitler'
s house at Berchtesgaden. This enraged Hitler to the
extent that he ordered her from the house and has had

little contact with her since. In any case, Adolph did not attend her second wedding.

Geli Raubal

Hitler's relationship with Geli, Angela's daughter, has already been described in the previous section. She died in 1930.

Leo Raubal

It has been generally assumed that Geli was the only child of Angela. William Patrick Hitler, however, reports that there is also a son named Leo. Not much is known of him except that he refused to have anything to do with his uncle Adolph after the death of Geli. He had a job in Salzburg and frequently came to Berchtesgaden to visit his mother when Hitler was in Berlin, but would leave again just as soon as word was received that Hitler was on his way there. According to William Patrick, he openly accused Hitler of causing Geli's death and refused to speak to him again as long as he lived. Word has been received that he was killed in 1942 while in the Balkans.

Paula Hitler

Paula Hitler, or Hiedler, is Adolph's real sister and is seven years younger. What happened to her after her mother's death is a mystery until she was discovered living very poorly in an attic in Vienna where she has a position addressing envelopes for an insurance company. She now lives under the name of Frau Wolf (Hitler's nickname is Wolf) and is alleged to be very queer and to receive no one in her home. Dr. Bloch went to visit her in the hope that she might intercede with her brother and obtain permission for him to take some money out of the country when he was exiled. He rapped on her door a number of times but received no answer. Finally, the neighbor on the same landing came to the door and asked who he was and what he wanted. The neighbor explained that Frau Wolf never received anyone and intimated that she was very queer (other writers have also reported this). She promised, however, to deliver any message he might give her. Dr. Bloch explained his predicament in detail. The next day when he returned, hoping that he would have an opportunity of speaking to Paula Hitler personally, the neighbor reported that Paula was very glad to hear from him and that she would do everything she could to help him. Nothing more.

During her childhood, according to William Patrick Hitler, she and Adolph did not get on very well together. There seems to have been considerable friction and jealousy between them, particularly since Alois Jr. was always taking her side. As far as is known, Hitler had no contact with her whatever from the time his mother died until 1955 when he became Chancellor. He has never mentioned her anywhere, as far as can be determined. It is alleged that he now sends her a small allowance each month to alleviate her poverty and keep her out of the limelight. According to William Patrick Hitler, his uncle became more interested in her as the friction with Angela increased. It is said that he has had her visit him at Berchtesgaden and William Patrick met her at the Bayreuth Festival in 1939 where she went by the name of Frau Wolf, but Hitler did not mention to anyone that it was his sister. He said she is a little on the stupid side and not very interesting to talk to since she rarely opens her mouth.

This is Adolph Hitler's family, past and present. It is possible that there is another sister, Ida, an imbecile, who is still living, but if so we have no knowledge of her whereabouts. On the whole, it is nothing to be proud of and Hitler may be wise in keeping it well under cover.

If we let our imaginations carry us back into the early '90s it is not difficult to picture what life was like for Adolph in his earliest years. His father was probably not much company for his mother. Not only was he twenty-three years older but, it seems, he spent most of his spare time in the taverns or gossiping with the neighbors. Furthermore, his mother knew only too well the past history of her husband, who was also her foster-father, and one can imagine that for a twenty-five year old woman this was not what might be called a romantic marriage. Moreover, Klara Hitler had lost her first two children, and possibly a third, in the course of three or four years. Then Adolph arrived. Under these circumstances, it is almost inevitable that he became the focal point in her life and that she left no stone unturned to keep him alive. All of the affection that normally would have gone to her husband and to her other children now became lavished on this newly born son.

It is safe to assume that for five years little Adolph was the center of attraction in this home. But then a terrible event happened in Adolph' s life - another son was born. No longer was he the center of attraction, no longer was he the king of the roost. The new-comer usurped all this and little Adolph, who was on his way to growing up, was left to shift more or less for himself - at least, so it probably seemed to him. Sharing was something he had not learned up to this time, and it was probably a bitter experience for him as it is for most children who have a sibling born when they are in this age period. In fact, in view of the earlier experiences of his parents it is reasonable to suppose that it was probably more acute in his case than it is with the average boy.

For two years he had to put up with this state of affairs. Then matters went from bad to worse - a baby sister was born. More competition and still less attention for the baby sister and the ailing brother were consuming all of his mother' s time while he was being sent off to school and made to take care of himself. Four years later tragedy again visited the Hitler household. When Adolph was eleven years old (in 1900) his baby brother, Edmund, died. Again we can imagine that Adolph reaped an additional harvest of affection and again became the apple of his mother's eye.

This is certainly an extraordinary series of events which must have left their mark on Adolph' s immature personality. What probably went on in his mind during these years we shall consider later on. It is sufficient at the moment to point out the extraordinary sequence of events and the probably [error in original document] effects they had on the members of the family and their relations with each other.

When Adolph was six years old he was sent off to school. The first school was a very small Volkschule where three grades met in the same room and were taught by the same teacher. In spite of the fact that he had to change schools several times in the course of the next few years, due to the fact that his father kept buying and selling his.property and moving from one place to another, he seems to have done quite well in his studies. When he was eight years old he attended a Benedict Monastery in Lamback. He was very much intrigued with all this - it gave him his first powerful impression of human achievement. At that time his ambition was to become an abbot. But things did not work out very well. He was dismissed from the monastery because he was caught smoking in the gardens. His last year in Volkschule was in Leonding where he received high marks in all his subjects with the occasional exception of singing, drawing and physical exercises.

In 1900, the year his brother Edmund died, he entered the Realschule in Linz. To the utter amazement of all who knew him his school work was so poor that he failed and had to repeat the class another time. Then there was a gradual improvement in his work, particularly in history, free-hand drawing and gymnastics. In these subjects he was marked "excellent" several times. Mathematics, French, German, etc., remained mediocre, sometimes satisfactory, sometimes unsatisfactory. On "Effort" he was frequently marked "irregular". When he was fourteen years of age his father died suddenly. The following year he left the Realschule in Linz and attended the one in Steyr. We do not know why this change was made. Dr. Bloch is under the impression that he was doing badly toward the end of the year in the Linz school and was sent to Steyr because it had the reputation of being easier. But his performance there was very mediocre. The only two subjects in which he excelled were in free-hand drawing, in which he was marked "praise-worthy" and gymnastics, in which he received the mark of "excellent". In the first semester "German Language" was "unsatisfactory" and in "History" it was "adequate".

All this is beautifully glossed over in Hitler's description of these years. According to his story he was at odds with his father concerning his future career as artist and in order to have his own way he sabotaged his studies - at least those he felt would not contribute to an artist's career, and History - which he says always fascinated him. In these studies, according to his own story he was always outstanding. An examination of his report cards reveals no such thing. History, even in his last year in Realschule is adequate or barely passing, and other subjects which might be useful to an artist are in the same category. A better diagnosis would be that he was outstanding in those subjects which did not require any preparation or thought while in those that required application he was sadly lacking. We frequently find report cards of this type among our patients who are very intelligent but refuse to work. They are bright enough to catch on to a few of the fundamental principles without exerting themselves and clever enough to amplify these sufficiently to obtain a passing-grade without ever doing any studying. They give the impression of knowing something about the subject but their knowledge is very superficial and is glossed over with glib words and terminology.

This evaluation of Hitler's school career fits in with the testimony of former fellow students and teachers. According to their testimony he never applied himself and was bored with what was going on. While the teacher was explaining new material, he read the books of Karl May (Indian and Wild West stories) which he kept concealed under his desk. He would come to school with bowie knives, hatchets, etc., and was always trying to initiate Indian games in which he was to be the leader. The other boys, however, were not greatly impressed by him and his big talk or his attempts to play the leader. On the whole, they preferred to follow the leadership of boys who were more socially-minded, more realistic in their attitudes - and held greater promise of future achievements than Hitler who gave every indication of being lazy, uncooperative, lived in a world of fantasy, talked big but did nothing of merit.

He probably did not improve his standing with the other boys when, in his twelfth year, he was found guilty of a "Sittlichkeitsvergehen" in the school. Just what the sexual indiscretion consisted of we do not know but Dr. Bloch, who remembers that one of the teachers in the school told him about it, feels certain that he had done something with a little girl. He was severely censured for this and barely missed being expelled from school. It is possible that he was ostracized by his fellow students and that this is the reason he changed schools the following year.

In September, 1905, he stopped going to school altogether and returned to Leonding where he lived with his mother and sister. According to his biographers, he was suffering from lung trouble during this period and had to remain in bed the greater part of the time. Dr. Bloch, who was the family doctor at this time is at a loss to understand how this story ever got started because there was no sign of lung trouble of any sort. Adolph came to his office now and then with a slight cold or a sore throat but there was nothing else wrong with him. According to Dr. Bloch, he was very quiet boy at this time, rather slight in build but fairly wiry. He was always very courteous and patiently waited for his turn. He made no fuss when the doctor looked into his throat or when he swabbed it with an antiseptic. He was very shy and had little to say except when spoken to. But there was no sign of lung trouble.

During this time, however, he frequently went with his mother to visit his aunt in Spital, Lower Austria where he also spent vacations. The doctor who treated him there is alleged to have said to the aunt: "From this illness Adolph will not recover." It is assumed that he referred to a lung condition but it seems that it must have been very slight because it was not reported to Dr. Bloch when he returned to Leonding a few months later and his records show no entry which would even suggest such an ailment.

Although the mother's income was extremely modest, he made no attempt to find work. There is some evidence that he went to a Munich art school for a short time during this period. Most of his time was evidently spent in loafing around and daubing paints and water colors. He took long walks into the hills, supposedly to paint, but it is reported that he was seen there delivering speeches to the rocks of the country in a most energetic tone of voice.

In October, 1807, he went to Vienna to prepare himself for the State examinations for admission as student to the Academy of Art. He qualified for admission to the examination but failed to be accepted as a student. On the first day of the examination the assignment was: "The Expulsion from Paradise" and on the second day: "An Episode of the Great Flood". The comment of the examiners was "Too few heads".

He returned home to Linz but there is no indication that he communicated to anybody the results of the examination. It was undoubtedly a severe blow to him for he tells us himself that he couldn't understand it, "he was so sure he would succeed." At this time his mother had already undergone an operation for cancer of the breast. She was failing rather rapidly and little hope was held for her recovery. She died on December 21, 1907 and was buried on Christmas Eve. To preserve a last impression,. he sketched her on her deathbed. Adolph, according to Dr. Bloch, was completely broken: "In all my career I have never seen anyone so prostrate with grief as Adolph Hitler." Although his sisters came to Dr. Bloch a few days after the funeral, and expressed themselves fully, Adolph remained silent. As the little group left, he said: "I shall be grateful to you forever." (29) After the funeral he stood at her grave for a long time after the sisters had left. The bottom had obviously fallen out of his world. Tears came into Dr. Bloch's eyes as he described the tragic scene. "His mother would turn over in her grave if she knew what he turned out to be." (21) This was the end of Adolph Hitler's family life.

LATER EXPERIENCES

VIENNA

Shortly after his mother's death the family broke up and Adolph went to Vienna to make his way in the world as his father had done before him. This was early in 1908. How much money, he took with him, if any, is not know [error in original document]. The records here are very vague particularly since all biographers have gone on the supposition that his mother died a year later than she actually did. This leaves an entire year unaccounted for since the next thing we hear of Adolph, he has again applied for admission to the examination for the Academy of Art. One of the conditions for re-examination was that he submit to the Board some of the paintings he had done previously. This he did but the Board was not impressed with them and refused to allow him to enter the examination. This, it seems, was even a greater shock than his failure to pass the examinations a year earlier.

After he had received notification to the effect that his work was of such a nature that it hid not warrant his admission to the second examination, he interviewed the Director. He claims that the Director, told him that his drawings showed clearly that his talents lay in the direction of architecture rather than pure art and advised him to seek admission to the Architectural School.

This he applied for but was not admitted. According to his story because he had not satisfactorily finished his course in the RealSchule. To be sure, this was one of the general requirements but exceptions could be made in the case of boys who showed unusual taIent. Hitler's rejection, therefore, was on the grounds of insufficient talent rather than for failure to complete his school course.

He was not without hope. All his dreams of being a great artist seemed to be nipped in the bud. He was without money and without friends. He was forced to go to work and found employment as a helper on construction jobs. This, however, did not suit him.

Hitler
As He Knows Himself

Part II

Friction developed between himself and his fellow workmen. It seems logical to suppose that he was working beneath his class and refused to mingle with them for he tells us that he sat apart from the others and ate his lunch. Further difficulties developed inasmuch as the workmen tried to convert him to a Marxian point of view. Their attitudes and arguments jarred him since they were far from the ideal Germany that had been portrayed by his favorite Linz teacher, Ludwig Poetsch, an ardent German nationalist. But Hitler found himself unable to answer their arguments. He made the unpleasant discovery that the workmen knew more than he did. He was fundamentaily against everything they said but he was unable to justify his point of view on an intellectual level – he was at a terrible disadvantage. In order to remedy the situation he began reading all kinds of political pamphlets and attending political meetings but not with the idea of understanding the problem as a whole, which might have enabled him to form an intelligent opinion, but to find arguments which would support his earlier conviction.

This is a trait that runs throughout his life. He never studies to learn but only to justify what he feels. In other words, his judgments are based wholly on emotionel factors and are then clothed with an intellectual argument. Soon, he tells us, he knew more than they did about their own political ideology and was able to tell them things about it which they did not know themselves.

It was this, according to Hitler, which antagonized the workmen against him. In one case, he was run off the job with the threat that if he appeared again they would push him off the scaffold. This must have been during the first half of 1909 when he was twenty years old. Without a job, he sunk lower and lower in the social scale and at times must have been on the verge of starvation. At times he found an odd job such as carrying luggage, shoveling snow or running errands but a large part of his time was spent in breadlines or begging on the streets.

In November, 1909, he was ousted from his room because he did not pay his rent and was forced to seek refuge in a flophouse. Here he met Reinhold Hanisch who was in much the same predicament. Years later, Hanisch wrote a long book about his associations with Hitler during this period. It is a gruesome story of unbelievable poverty. Hltler must have been a sorry sight during these days with a full black beard, badly clothed and a haggard look. Hanisch writes:

> "It was a miserable life and I once asked him what he was really waiting for. The answer: 'I don't know myself'. I have never seen such hopeless letting down in distress."

Hanisch took him in hand end encouraged him to do some

painting. The difficulty was that neither one had the money with which to buy materials. When Hanisch discovered that Hitler had signed over his inheritance to his sister, he persuaded Hitler to write her and obtain a small loan. This was presumably his half-sister, Angela. When the money was received Hitler's first thought was to take week's vacation in order to recuperate. At this time he moved into the Maennerheim Brigittenau which was slightly better than the flophouses in which he had been staying.

He and Hanisch went into business together. It was Hitler's job to paint post cards, posters and water-colors which Hanisch then took around Vienna and peddled to art dealers, furniture stores, etc. In this he was quite successful but his difficultes were not at an end. The moment Hitler got a little money, he refused to work. Hanisch describes this beautifully:

"But unfortunately Hitler was never an ardent worker. I often was driven to despair by bringing in orders that he simply wouldn't carry out. At Easter, 1910, we earned forty kronen on a big order and we divided it equally. The next morning, when I came downstairs and asked for Hitler, I was told he had already left with Neumann, a Jew.... After that I couldn't find him for a week. He was sightseeing Vienna with Neumann and spent much of the time in the museum. When I asked him what the matter was and whether we were going to keep on working, he answered that he must recuperate now, that he must have some leisure, that he was not a coolie. When the week was over, he had no longer any money."

At this time, Hitler was not a Jew-hater. There were a number of Jews living in the Mne's Home with whom he was on excellent terms. Most of his paintingss were sold to Jewish dealers who paid just as much for them as the Aryans, He also admired Rothschild for sticking to his religion even if it prevented him from entering court. During this time he also sent two postcards to Dr. Bloch, in Linz, who was s Jew. One of these was just a picture postcard of Vienna; the other, a copy which he had painted. On both of them he wrote of his deep gratitude to the doctor. This is mentioned because it is one of the very few cases of which we have any record in which Hitler showed any lasting gratitude. During this time Hitler himself looked very Jewish. Hanisch writes:

> "Hitler at that time looked very Jewish, so that I often joked with him that he must be of Jewish blobd, since such a large beard rarely grows on a Christian's chin. Also he had big feet, as a desert wanderer must have."

In spite of his close association with Hanisch the relationship ended in a quarrel. Hitler accused Hanisch of withholding some of the money he had received for a picture. He had Hanisch arrested and appeared as a witness against him. We have little knowledge of what happened to Hitler after this time. According to Hanfstaengl the home in which Hitler lived has a reputation of being a place where homosexual men frequently went to find companions. Jahm said that he had information from a Viennese official that on the police record Hitler was listed as a sexual pervert but it gave no details of offenses. It is possible that the entry may have been made solely on suspicion.

Simone (467) claims that the Viennese police file in 1912 recorded a charge of theft against Hitler and that he moved from Vienna to Munich in order to avoid arrest. This would fit in with Hanfstaengl's suspicion that Hitler's elder half-brother (who was twice convicted for theft) was in Vienna at that time and that they may have become involved in some minor crime. This would not be impossible for Hanisch tells us that Hitler frequently spent his time figuring out shady ways of making money. One example may be of interest:

"He proposed to fill old tin-cans with paste
and sell them to shopkeepers, the paste to
be smeared on windowpanes to keep them from
freezing in winter.' It should be sold.... in
the summer, when it couldn't be tried out. I
told him it wouldn't work because the merchants
would just say, come back in the winter....
Hitler answered that one must possess a talent
for oratory."

Since Hitler could only be brought to work when he was
actually hungry he spent a good deal of time reading
political pamphlets, sitting in care houses, reading
newspapers and delivering speeches to the other inmates
of the home. He became a great admirer of Georg von
Schoenerer and the Viennese mayor, Karl Lueger. It was
presumably from them that he learned his anti-Semitism
and many of the tricks of a successful politician.
According to Hanisch his companions were greatly amused
by him and often ridiculed him and his opinions. In
any event it seems that he got a good deal of practice
in speech making during these years which stood him in
good stead later on. Even in these days, he talked about
starting a new party.

It is not clear why he remained in Vienna and lived in
such poverty for five years, when he had such a deep love
for Germany and could have gone there with relatively
little difficulty. It is also not clear why he went when
he did unless there is some truth in the supposition
that he fled Vienna to avoid arrest. His own explanation
is that he could not tolerate the mixture of people,
particularly the Jews and always more Jews, and says
that for him Vienna is the symbol of incest.

But as far as Hitler is concerned this time was not
lost. As he looks back over that period he can say:

"So in a few years I built a foundation of
knowledge from which I still draw nourishment
today." (MK 29)

"At that time I formed an image of the world and a view of life which became the granite foundation for my actions."

PRE-WAR MUNICH:

In Munich before the war, things were no better for him. As far as poverty is concerned he might as well have stayed in Vienna. He earned a little money painting postcards and posters and at times painting houses. Early in 1913 he went to Salzburg to report for duty in the army but was rejected on the gr.unds of poor physical conition. He returned to Munich and continued to work at odd jobs and sit in cafe houses where he spent his time reading newspapers. Nothing of which we have any knowledge happened during this time which is particularly pertinent to our present study. The prospects of ever making anything out of himself in the future must have been very black at that time.

WORLD WAR:

Then came the World War. He writes of this occasion:

> "The struggle of the year 1914 was forsooth, not forced on the masses, but desired by the whole people."

> "To myself those hours came like a redemption from the vexatious experiences of my youth. Even,to this day I am not ashamed to say that, in a transport of enthusiasm, I sank down on my knees and thanked Heaven from an overflowing heart...."

On August 3, 1914, Hitler joined a Bavarian regiment as a volunteer. During the first days of the war his regiment suffered very heavy losses and was not particularly popular among the Bavarian people. Hitler became an orderly in Regimental Headquarters as well as a runner. The one thing that all his comrades commented on was his subservience to superior officers. It seems that he went out of his way to court their good graces, offering to do their washing and other menial tasks much to the disgust of his comrades. He was not popular with the other men and always remained aloof from them. When he did join them he usually harangued about political matters.

During the four years of war he received no packages or mail from anyone. In this he was unique. At Christmastime when everyone else was receiving gifts and messages he withdrew from the group and sulked moodily by himself. When his comrades encouraged him to join the group and share their packages he refused. On October 7, 1916, he was wounded by a piece of shrapnel and sent to a hospital. It was a light wound and he was soon discharged and sent to Munich as a replacement. After two days there he wrote his commanding officer, Captain Wiedemann, asking that he be reinstated in his regiment because he could not tolerate Munich when he knew his comrades were at the Front. Wiedemann had him returned to the regiment where he remained until October 14th when he was exposed to mustard gas and sent to a hospital in Pasewalk. He was blind and, according to Friedelinde Wagner, lost his voice.

It seems that mystery always follows Hitler. His career in the army is no exception. There are several things that have never been satisfactorily explained. The first is that he spent four years in the same regiment but was never advanced beyond the rank of First Class Private or Lance Corporal. The second is the Iron Cross First Class which he constantly wears. This has been the topic of much discussion but the mystery has never been solved. There is no mention of the award in the history of his regiment. This is rather amazing inasmuch as other awards of this kind are listed. Hitler is mentioned, in a number of other connections but not in this one, although it is alleged that it was awarded to him for capturing twelve Frenchmen, including an officer, singlehanded. This is certainly no ordinary feat in any regiment and one would expect that it would at least merit some mention, particularly in view of the fact that Hitler had considerable fame as a politician when the book went to press.

The Nazi propaganda agencies have not helped to clarify the situation. Not only have a number of different versions of the story appeared in the press, but each gives a different number of Frenchmen he is alleged to have captured. They have also published alleged facsimiles of his war record which do not agree. The Berlin Illustrierte Zeitung of August 10, 1939 printed a facsimile in which the date of award for this decoration was clearly August 4, 1918. Yet the Voelkische Beobachter of August 14, 1934 had published a facsimile in which the date of award was October 4, 1918. Although these alleged facsimiles mentioned other citations they did not include the date of award of the Iron Cross Second Class. From all that can be learned the First Class Cross was never awarded unless the recipient had already been awarded the Second Class decoration.

Just what the facts are it is impossible to determine. It is alleged that his war record has been badly tampered with and that von Schleicher was eliminated during the Blood Purge because he knew the true facts. Strasser who served in the same division has probably as good an explanation as any. He says that during the last months of the war there were so many First Class Crosses being given out that General Headquarters was no longer able to pass on the merits of each individual case. To facilitate matters a number of these decorations were allotted to each regiment every month to be issued by the Commanding Officers. They, in turn, notified the High Command of the award and the deed which merited it. According to Strasser, when the army began to collapse, the Regimental Headquarters had in their possession a number of decorations which had not been awarded.

Since few members of the Headquarters Staff ever received an award of this type they took advantage of the general melee and gave them to each other and forged the signatures of the commanding officer in sending it to the High Command. The thing that speaks in favor of this explanation is the curious bond which exists between Hitler and his regimental sergeant-major, Max Areann who was later to become the head of the Nazi Eher Verlag. This is one of the most lucrative positions in the entire Nazi hierarchy and Amann was called to the position by Hitler.

The only explanation for the lack of promotion that has been published is the comment of one of his officers to the effect that he would never make a non-commissioned officer "out of that neurotic fellow, Hitler". Rauschning (947) gives a different explanation. He claims that a high Nazi had once confided in him that he had seen Hitler's military record and that it contained an item of a court martial which found him guilty of pederastic practices with an officer, and that it was for this reason that he was never promoted. Rauschning also claims that in Munich Hitler was found guilty of a violation of paragraph 175 which deals with pederasty. No other evidence of either of these two charges has been found.

The mystery becomes even deeper when we learn from a great many informants that Hitler was quite courageous and never tried to evade dangerous assignments, It is said that he was unusually adept at running and then falling or seeking shelter when the fire became intense. It also seems that he was always ready to volunteer for special assignments and was considered exceedingly reliable in the performance of all his duties by his own officers.

It may be well to mention at this point that when Hitler entered the army he again became a member of a recognized and respected social institution. No longer did he have to stand in breadlines or seek shelter in flophouses, For the first time since his mother died did he really belong to a group of people. Not only did this provide him with a sense of pride and security but at last he had achieved his great ambition, namely, to be united with the German nation. It is also interesting to note a considerable change in his appearance. From the dirty, greasy, cast-off clothes of Jews and other charitable people he was now privileged to wear a uniform. Mend (209), one of his comrades, tells us that when Hitler came out of the trenches or back from an assignment he spent hours cleaning his uniform and boots until he became the joke of the regiment. Quite a remarkable change for one who for almost seven years refused to exert himself just a little in order to pull himself out of the pitiful conditions in which he lived among the dregs of Society.

POST-WAR

Then came the armistice and all this was over. Adolph Hitler from a psychological point of view, was in exactly the same position as the one in which he found himself eleven years before when his mother died. He faced the future alone. The army, his home for four years, was breaking up. Again he stood alone before a dismal future - a world in which he could not find a niche, a world which did not care for him, a world of aimless existence fraught with hardships. It was more than he could face.

Where to go and what to do. Having no home or family to greet him he returned to Munich not because it had been kind to him in the past but because he had no other

place to go. He could take up his life again where he had left off four years earlier. He wandered around Munich for a short time "a stray dog looking for a master". Then it is reported that he went to Vienna to visit his halfsister, Angela, with whom he had had contact for many years. If he actually. made this trip he did not stay long for soon we find him in the reserve army, stationed in Traunstein. He is in a deep depression. He wears the uniform and eats the food of the army. It is his only recourse and he stays on there in this capacity until April, 1920, when the camp is broken up. He then returned to Munich still attached to the army and living in the barracks. During this time he seems to have continued his political discussions with his comrades siding with the Social Democrats against the Communists. According to the Muenchener Post he actually affiliated himself with the Social Democratic Party (483). After the counter-revolution every tenth man in the barracks was shot but Hitler was singled out beforehand and asked to stand one side. At the inquiry he appeared before the board with "charge-lists" against some of his comrades which can only signify denunciations for Communistic activities. He had been spying on his comrades and now assigned them to the executiener. In MEIN KAMPF he refers to this occupation as his "first more or less political activity".

The Army now undertook to educate its soldiers in the proper political philosophy and Hitler was assigned to such a course. He spoke so ably in this group that his talent for speaking impressed an officer who was presents and Hitler was appointed "education officer". His hour had struck - he was discovered and appreciated, singled out for his talent. He threw himself into this work with great enthusiasm always speaking to larger groups. His confidence grew with his success in swaying people. He was on his way to become a politician. From here on his career is a matter of history and need not be reviewed here.

This is the foundation of Hitler's character. Whatever he tried to be afterwards is only super-structure and the super-structure can be no firmer than the foundations on which it rests. The higher it goes the more unstable it becomes - the more it needs to be propped up and patched up in order to make it hold together. This is not an easy job. It requires constant vigilance, strong defenses and heavy losses in time and energy.

There was unanimous agreement among the four psychoanalysts who have studied the material that Hitler is an hysteric bordering on schizophrenia and not a paranoiac as is so frequently supposed. This means that he is not insane in the commonly accepted sense of the term, but neurotic. He has not lost complete contact with the world about him and is still striving to make some kind of psychological adjustment which will give him a feeling of security in his social group. It also means that there is a definite moral component in his character no matter how deeply it may be buried or how seriously it has been distorted.

With this diagnosis established, we are in a position to make a number of surmises concerning the conscious mental processes which ordinarily take place in Hitler's mind. These form the nucleus of the "Hitler"; he consciously knows and must live with. It is in all probability not a happy "Hitler" but one harrassed by fears, anxieties, doubts, misgivings, uncertainties, condemnations, feelings of loneliness and of guilt. From our experience with other hysterics we are probably on firm ground when we suppose that Hitler's mind is like a "battle-royal" most of the time with many conflicting and contradictory forces and impulses pulling him this way and that.

Such a state of confusion is not easy to bear. His energies are absorbed in wrestling with himself instead of striving for gratifications in the external world which he wants and needs. He sees the possibilities all around him but he can rarely muster enough energy to make the effort to go after them. Fears, doubts and implications obstruct his thinking and acting and he becomes indecisive and winds up doing nothing but wishing. Vicarious gratifications through fantasies become substitutes for the satisfaction obtained from real achievements. We must suppose that this is the state that Hitler was in during the seven years that elapsed between the death of his mother and the outbreak of the war when he was wasting his time lying around in flophouses and sitting in cafes in Vienna. Only when his hunger became acute could he muster the energy necessary to apply himself to a few hours of work. As soon as this hunger was appeased he lapsed back into his former state of procrastination and indecision.

We must assume that that the periods of procrastination at the present time have a similar origin. He. withdraws from society, is depressed and dawdles away his time until "the situation becomes dangerous" then he forces himself to action. He works for a time and as soon as the job is underway "he loses interest in it" and slips back into his leisurely life in which he does nothing except what he is forced to do or likes to do. Now, of course, it is no longer hunger that drives him to work but another motive, even more powerful, of which he is not fully conscious. The nature of this motive will be discussed in the next section.

As one surveys Hitler's behavior patterns, as his close associates observe them, one gets the distinct impression that this is not one person but two which inhabit the same body and alternate back and forth. The one is a very soft, sentimental and indecisive individual who has little drive and wants nothing quite so much as to be amused, liked and looked after. The other is just the opposite - hard, cruel and decisive with an abundant reservoir of energy at his command - who knows what he wants and is ready to go after it and get it regardless of costs. It is the first Hitler who weeps profusely at the death of his canary, and the second Hitler who cries in open court: "Heads will roll". It is the first Hitler who cannot bring himself to discharge an assistant and it is the second Hitler who can order the murder of hundreds including his best friends and can say with great conviction: "There will be no peace in the land until a body hangs from every lamp-post". It is the first Hitler who spends his evenings watching movies or going cabarets and it is the second Hitler who works for days on end with little or no sleep, making plans which will affect the destiny of nations.

Until we understand the magnitude and implications of this duality in his nature we can never understand his actions. It is a kind of "Dr. Jekyll and Mr. Hyde" personality structure in which two wholly different, radical oscillations take place and make the person almost unrecognizable. This characteristic, too, is common to many hysterics. Under these circumstances it is extremely difficult to predict from moment to moment what his reactions to a given situation are going to be. An illustration may be helpful. According to Russell (746) extravagant preparations were made for the commemorative services for the Germans who died when the battleship Deutschland was bombed. Hitler spoke long and passionately to those attending, as well as over the radio. It was then arranged that he should walk down the line of survivors and review the infantry and naval units drawn up at attention. Newsreel cameramen were stationed at all crucial points:

> "The first widow to whom Hitler spoke a few words cried violently. Her child, who was 10 years old and who stood next to his bereaved mother, began to cry heartrendingly. Hitler patted him on the head and turned uncertainly to the next in line. Before he could speak a word, he was suddenly overcome. He spun completely around, left the carefully prepared program flat. Followed by his utterly surprised companions he walked as fast as he could to his car and had himself driven away from the parade grounds."

This sudden alternation from one to the other is not uncommon. Close asociates have commented on it time and time again. Ludecke (166) writes:

> "There were times when he gave an impression of unhappiness, of loneliness, of inward searching .... But in a moment, he would turn again to whatever frenzied task with the swift command of a man born for action."

Rauschning (263):

> "Almost anything might suddenly inflame his wrath and hatred .... But equally, the transition from

anger to sentimentality or enthusiasm might be quite sudden."

Huddleston (759) writes:

"His eyes, soft and dreamy as he spoke to me, suddenly flashed and hardened..."

Voight (591) says:

"Close collaborators for many years said that Hitler was always like this – the slightest difficulty or obstacle could make him scream with rage or burst into tears."

Heiden has commented upon the duality of Hitler's character and has suggested that the procrastinating side is "Hitler" while the fiery personality which erupts from time to time is the Fuehrer. Although this may not be strictly true from a psychological point of view, it may be helpful to think of them in these terms.

There is not, however, a complete dissociation of the personality. In such a case we would expect to find the personalities alternating with each other quite beyond the voluntary control of the individual. This is clearly not the case with Hitler who can adopt either role more or less at will. At least, he is able, on occasion, to induce the Fuehrer personality to come into existence when the occasion demands. This is what he does at almost every speech. At the beginning as we have mentioned he is nervous and insecure on the platform. At times he has considerable difficulty in finding anything to say. This is "Hitler". But under these circumstances the "Hitler" personality does not usually predominate for any length of time. As soon as he gets the feel of the audience the tempo of the speech increases and the "Fuehrer" personality begins to assert itself. Heiden says: "The stream of speech stiffens him like a stream of water stiffens a hose." As he speaks he seduces himself into believing that he is actually and fundamentally the "Fuehrer", or as Rausching (268) says: "He doses himself with the morphine of his own verbiage." It is this transformation, of the little Hitler into the great Fuehrer, which takes place under the eyes of his audience which probably fascinates them. By complicated psychological processes they are able to identify themselves with him and as the speech progresses, they themselves are temporarily transformed and inspired.

He must also undergo a transformation of this kind when he is expected to make a decision or take definite action. As we have seen, Hitler procrastinates until the situation becomes dangerous and intolerable. When he can procrastinate no longer, he is able to induce the Fuehrer personality to assert itself. Rauschning has put this well:

> "He is languid and apathetic by nature and needs the stimulus of nervous excitement to rouse him out of chronic lethargy to a spasmodic activity." (269)

> "Before Hitler can act he must lash himself out of lethargy and doubts into a frenzy." (262)

Having lashed himself into this state of mind he can play the "Fuehrer" to perfection. When the transformation takes place in his personality all his views, sentiments and values are also transformed. The result is that as "Fuehrer" he can make statements with great conviction which flatly contradict what "Hitler" said a few minutes earlier. He can grapple with the most important problems and in a few minutes reduce them to extremely simple terms, he can map out campaigns, be the supreme judge, deal with diplomats, ignore all ethical and moral principles, order executions, or the destruction of cities without the slightest hesitation. And he can be in the best of humor while he is doing it. All of this would have been completely impossible for "Hitler".

Hitler likes to believe that this is his true self and

he has made every effort to convince the German people that it is his only self. But it is an artiface. The whole "Fuehrer" personality is a grossly exaggerated and distorted conception of masculinity as Hitler conceives it. Undoubtedly he would like to be such a person in reality and believes that he actually is that person - but he deceives himself. This personality shows all the ear-marks of a reaction formation which has been created unconsciously as a compensation and cover-up for deeplying [error in original document] tendencies which he despises. This mechanism is very frequently found in hysterics and always serves the purpose of denying the true self by creating an image which is diametrically opposite and then identifying with the image. The great difference between Hitler and thousands of other hysterics is that he managed to convince millions of other people that the image is really himself. The more he was able to convince them, the more he became convinced of it himself on the theory that eighty million Germans can't be wrong.

And so he has fallen in love with the image he, himself, created and does his utmost to forget that behind it there is quite another Hitler who is a very despicable fellow.

He is hardly more successful in this, manouvre than any other hysteric. Secret fears and anxieties that belie the reality of the image keep cropping up to shake his confidence and security. He may rationalize these fears or displace them but they continue to haunt him. Underneath, Hitler is a bundle of fears. Some are at least partially justified, others seem to be groundless. For example, he has had a fear of cancer for many years. Ordinarily he fears that he has a cancer in his stomach since he is always bothered with indigestion. The assurances of his doctors are all to no avail. A few years ago a simple polyp grew on his larynx. Immediately his fear shifted to the throat and he was sure that he had developed a throat cancer. When Dr. von Eicken diagnosed it as a simple polyp, Hitler at first refused to believe him.

Then he has fears of being poisoned, fears of being assassinated, fears of losing his health, fears of gaining weight, fears of treason, fears of losing his mystical guidance, fears of anesthetics, fears of premature death, fears that his mission will not be fulfilled, etc. Every conceivable precaution must be taken to reduce these dangers, real and imagined, to a minimnm. In later years, the fear of betrayal and possible assassination by one of his associates seems to have grown considerably. Thyssen (308) claims that it has reached the point where he no longer trusts the Gestapo. Frank (652) reports that even the generals must surrender their swords before they are admitted into conferences with him.

Sleep is no longer a refuge from his fears. He wakes up in the night shaking and screaming. Rauschning claims that one of Hitler's close associates told him that:

> "Hitler wakes at night with convulsive shrieks; shouts for help. He sits on the edge of his bed, as if unable to stir. He shakes with fear, making the whole bed vibrate. He shouts confused, unintelligible phrases. He gasps, as if imagining himself to be suffocating. On one occasion Hitler, stood swaying in his room, looking wildly about him. 'He! He! He's been here!' he gasped. His lips were blue. Sweat streamed down his face. Suddenly he began to reel off figures, and odd words and broken phrases, entirely devoid of sense. It sounded horrible. He used strangely composed and entirely un-German word-formations. Then he stood still, only his lips moving... Then he suddenly broke out 'There, there!' In the corner! Who's that?' He stamped and shrieked in the familiar way."

Zeissler (923), also reports such incidents. It would seem that Hitler's late hours are very likely due to the fact that he is afraid to go to sleep.

The result of these fears, as it is with almost every hysteric, is a narrowing of the world in which he lives. Haunted by these fears, he distrusts everyone, even those closest to him. He cannot establish any close friendships for fear of being betrayed or being discovered as he really is. As his world becomes more and more circumscribed he becomes lonelier and lonelier. He feels himself to be a captive and often compares his life with that of the Pope (Hanfstaengl, 912). Fry (577) says, "spiritual loneliness must be Hitler's secret regret", and von Wiegand (491) writes:

> "Perhaps the snow-crowned peaks of the Alps glistening in the moonlight remind Adolph Hitler of the glittering but cold, lonely heights of fame and achievement to which he has climbed. 'I am the loneliest man on earth' he said to an employee of his household. '"

Hysterics, however, are not discouraged by all this. On the contrary, they interpret their fears as proof of their own importance rather than as signs of their fundamental weakness. As Hitler's personal world becomes smaller he must extend the boundaries of his physical domains. Meanwhile, his image of himself must become evermore inflated in order to compensate for his deprivations and the maintenance of his repressions. He must build bigger and better buildings, bridges, stadia and what not, as tangible symbols of his power and greatness and then use these as evidence that he really is what he wants to believe he is.

There is, however, little gratification in all this. No matter what he achieves or what he does it is never sufficient to convince him that things are what they seem to be. He is always insecure and must bolster up his super-structure by new acquisitions and more defenses. But the more he gets and the higher he builds, the more he has to worry about and defend. He is caught in a vicious circle, like so many other hysterics, which grows bigger and bigger as time goes on but never brings them the sense of security they crave above everything else.

The reason for this is that they are barking up the wrong tree. The security they seek is not to be found in the outside world but in themselves. Had they conquered their own unsocial impulses, their real enemy, when they were young, they would not need to struggle with such subterfuges when they are mature. The dangers they fear in the world around them are only the shadows of the dangers they fear will creep up on them from within if they do not maintain a strict vigilance over their actions. Denying does not annihilate them. Like termites, they gnaw away at the foundation of the personality and the higher the super-structure is built, the shakier it becomes.

In most hysterics, these unsocisl impulses, which they regard as dangers, have been fairly successfully repressed. The individual feels himself to be despicable without being conscious of the whys and wherefores of this feeling. The origins of the feeling remain almost wholly unconscious or are camouflaged in such a way that they are not obvious to the individual himself. In Hitler's case, this is not so - at least not entirely. He has good cause for feeling despicable and he knows why. The repression in his case was not completely successful and some of the unsocial tendencies do from time to time assert themselves and demand satisfaction.

Hitler's sexual life has always been the topic of much speculation. As pointed out in the previous section, ZZZ of his closest associates are absolutely ignorant on this subject. This has led to conjectures of all sorts. Some believe that he is entirely immune from such impulses. Some believe that he is a chronic masturbator. Some believe that he derives his sexual pleasure through voyeurism. Many believe that he is completely impotent. Others, and these are perhaps in the majority, that he is homosexual. It is probably true that he is impotent but he is certainiy not homosexual in the ordinary sense of the term. His perversion has quite a different nature which few have guessed. He is an extreme masochist who derives sexual pleasure from having a woman squat over him while she uriniates or defecates on his face. (Strasser, 919; see also 931, 932)*

Although this perversion is not a common one, it is not unknown in clinical work, particularly in its incipient stages. The four collaborators on this study, in addition to Dr. De Saussure who learned of the perversion from other sources, have all had experience with cases of this type. All five agree that their information as given is probably true in view of their clinical experience and their knowledge of Hitler's character. In the following section further evidence of its validition will be cited. At the present moment it is sufficient to recognize the influence that this perversion must have on the conscious mental life of Hitler.

Unquestionably Hitler has suffered severe guilt reactions

> *Note: There may be some people who would question the reliability of any information given by Otto Strasser because of his reputation. It is perhaps because of his reputation that he came by this information which had been so carefully guarded. He also supplied the interviewer with a great deal of other information concerning Hitler which checked very closely with that of other informants. As far as this study is concerned we have no reason to question his sincerity.

from his perverse tendencies. We can easily imagine interminable struggles with his conscience which incapacitated him to a considerable extent. Surely Hitler has externalized his own problem and its supposed solution when he writes:

"Only when the time comes when the race is no longer overshadowed by the consciousness of its own guilt, then it will find internal peace and external energy to cut down regardlessly and brutally the wild shoots, and to pull up the weeds."

and again:

"We must be ruthless....We must regain our clear conscience as to ruthlessness.... Only thus shall we purge our people of their softness and sentimental Philistinism, and their degenerate delight in beer swilling."

Hitler
Psychological Analysis & Reconstruction

Part I

The world has come to know Adolph Hitler for his insatiable greed for power, his ruthlessness, cruelty and utter lack-of feeling, his contempt for established institutions and his lack of moral restraints. In the course of relatively few years he has contrived to usurp such tremendous power that a few veiled threats, accusations or insinuations were sufficient to make the world tremble. In open defiance of treaties he occupied huge territories and conquered millions of people without even firing a shot. When the world became tired of being frightened and concluded that it was all a bluff, he initiated the most brutal and devastating war in history - a war which, for a time, threatened the complete destruction of our civilization. Human life and human suffering seem to leave this individual completely untouched as he plunges along the course he believes he was predestined to take.

Earlier in his career the world had watched him with amusement. Many people refused to take him seriously on the grounds that "he could not possibly last." As one action after another met with amazing success and the measure of the man became more obvious, this amusement was transformed into incredulousness. To most people it seemed inconceivable that such things could actually happen in our modern civilization. Hitler, the leader of these activities, became generally regarded as a madman, if not inhuman. Such a conclusion, concerning the nature of our enemy, may be satisfactory from the point of view of the man in the street. It gives him a feeling of satisfaction to pigeon-hole an incomprehensible individual in one category or another. Having classified him in this way, he feels that the problem is completely solved. All we need to do is to eliminate the madman from the scene of activities, replace him with a sane individual, and the world will again return to a normal and peaceful state of affairs.

This naive view, however, is wholly inadequate for those who are delegated to conduct the war against Germany or for those who will be delegated to deal with the situation when the war is over. They cannot content themselves with simply regarding Hitler as a personal devil and condemning him to an Eternal Hell in order that the remainder of the world may live in peace and quiet. They will realize that the madness of the part of wholly the actions of a single individual but that a reciprocal relationship exists between the Fuehrer and the people and that the madness of the one stimulates and flows into the other and vice versa. It was not only Hitler, the madman, who created German madness, but German madness which created Hitler. Having created him as its spokesman and leader, it has been carried along by his momentum, perhaps far beyond the point where it was originally prepared to go. Nevertheless, it continues to follow his lead in spite of the fact that it must be obvious to all intelligent people now that his path leads to inevitable destruction.

Dissecting the Hitler Mind

From a scientific point of view, therefore, we are forced to consider Hitler, the Fuehrer, not as a personal devil, wicked as his actions and philosophy may be, but as the expression of a state of mind existing in millions of people, not only in Germany but, to a smaller degree, in all civilized countries. To remove Hitler may be a necessary first step, but it would not be the cure. It would be analogous to curing an ulcer without treating the underlying disease. If similar eruptions are to be prevented in the future, we cannot content ourselves with simply removing the overt manifestations of the disease. On the contratry, we must ferret out and seek to correct the underlying factors which produced the unwelcome phenomenon. We must discover the psychological streams which nourish this destructtve state of mind in order that we may divert them into channels which will permit a further evolution of our form of civilization.

The present study is concerned wholly with Adolph Hitler and the social forces which impinged upon him in the course of his development and produced the man we know. One may question the wisdom of studying the psychology of a single individual if the present war represents a rebellion by a nation against our civilization. To understand the one does not tell us anything about the millions of others. In a sense this is perfectly true. In the process of growing up we are all faced with highly individual experiences and exposed to varying social influences. The result is that when we mature no two of us are identical from a psychological point of view. In the present instance, however, we are concerned not so much with distinct individuals as with a whole cultural group. The members of this group have been exposed to social influences, family patterns, methods of training and education, opportunities for development, etc., which are fairly homogeneous within a given culture or strata of a culture. The result is that the members of a given culture tend to act, think and feel more or less alike, at least in contrast to the members of a different cultural group. This justifies, to some extent, our speaking of a general cultural character.

On the other hand, if a large section of a given culture rebells against the traditional pattern then we must assume that new social influences have been introducod which tend to produce a type of character which cannot thrive in the old cultural environment.

When this happens it may be extremely helpful to understand the nature of the social forces which influenced the development of individual members of the group. These may serve as clues to an understanding of the group as a whole inasmuch as we can then investigate the frequency and intensity of these same forces in the group as a whole and draw deductions concerning their effect upon its individual members. If the individual being studied happens to be the Ieader of the group, we can expect to find the pertinent factors in an exaggerated form which would tend to make them stand out in sharper relief than would be the case if we studied an average member of the group. Under these circumstances, the action of the forces may be more easily isolated and subjected to detailed study in relation to the personality as whole as well as to the culture in general. The problem of our study should be, then, not only whether Hitler is mad or not, but what influences in his development have made him what he is.

If we scan the tremendous quantities of material and information which have been accumulated on Hitler, we find little which is helpful in explaining why he is what he is. One can, of course, make general statements as many authors have done and say, for example, that his five years in Vienna were so frustrating that he hated the whole social order and is now taking his revenge for the injustices he suffered. Such explanations sound very plausible at first glance but we would also want to know why, as a young man, he was unwilling to work when he had the opportunity and what happened to transform the lazy Vienna beggar into the energetic politician who never seemed to tire from rushing from one meeting to another and was able to work thousands of listeners into a state of frenzy.

We would also like to know something about the origins of his peculiar working habits at the present time, his firm belief in his mission, and so on. No matter how long we study the available material we can find no rational explanation of his present conduct. The material is descriptive and tells us a great deal about how he behaves under varying circumstances, what he thinks and feels shout various subjects, but it does not tell us why. To be sure, he himself sometimes offers explanations for his conduct but it is obvious that these are either built on flimsy rational foundations or else they serve to push the problem further back into his past. On this level we are in exactly the same position in which we find ourselves when a neurotic patient first comes for help.

In the case of an individual neurotic patient, however, we can ask for a great deal more first-hand information which gradually enables us to trace the development of his irrational attitudes or behavioral patterns to earlier experiences or influences in his life history and the effects of these on his later behavior. In most cases the patient will have forgotten these earlier experiences but nevertheless he still uses them as premises in his present conduct. As soon as we are able to understand the premises underlying his conduct, then his irrational behavior becomes comprehensible to us.

The same finding would probably hold in Hitler's case except that here we do not have the opportunity of obtaining the additional first-hand information which would enable us to trace the history of his views and behavioral patterns to their early origins in order to discover the premises on which he is operating. Hitler's early life, when his fundamental attitudes were undoubtedly formed, is a closely guarded secret, particularly as far as he himself is concerned. He has been extremely careful and has told us exceedingly little about this period of his life and even that is open to serious questioning. A few fragments have, however, been, unearthed which are helpful in reconstructing his past life and the experiences and influences which have determined his adult character. Nevertheless, in themselves, they would be wholly inadequate for our purposes.

Fortunately, there are other sources of information. One of them is Hitler himself. In every utterance a speaker or writer unknowingly tells us a great deal about himself of which he is entirely unaware. The subjects he chooses for elaboration frequently reveal unconscious factors which make these seem more important to him than many other aspects which would be just as appropriate to the occasion. Furthermore, the method of treatment, together with the attitudes expressed towards certain topics, usually reflect conscious processes which are symbolically related to his own problems. The examples he chooses for purposes of illustration almost always contain elements from his own earlier experiences which were instrumental in cultivating the view he is expounding. The figures of speech he employs reflect unconscious conflicts and linkages and the incidence of particular types or topics can almost be used as a measure of his preoccupation with problems related to them. A number of experimental techniques have been worked out which bear witness to the validity of these methods of gathering information about the mental life, conscious and unconscious, of an individual in addition to the findings of psychoanalysts and psychiatrists.

Then, too, we have our practical experience in studying patients whose difficulties were not unlike those we find in Hitler. Our knowledge of the origins of these difficulties may often be used to evaluate conflicting information, check deductions concerning what probably happened, or to fill in gaps where no information is available. It may be possible with the help of all these sources of information to reconstruct the outstanding events in his early life which have determined his present behavior and character structure. Our study must, however, of necessity be speculative and inconclusive. It may tell us a great deal about the mental processes of our subject but it cannot be as comprehensive or conclusive as the findings of a direct study conducted with the cooperatlon of the individual. Nevertheless, the situation is such that even an indirect study of this kind is warranted.

Freud's earliest and greatest contribution to psychiatry in particular and to an understanding of human conduct in general was his discovery of the importance of the first years of a child's life in shaping his future character. It is during these early years, when the child's acquaintanceship with the world is still meagre and his capacities are still immature, that the'chances of misinterpreting the nature of the world about him are the greatest. The mind of the child is inadequate for understanding the demands which a complex culture makes upon him or the host of confusing experiences to which he is exposed. In consequence, as has been shown over and over again, a child during his early years frequently misinterprets what is going on about him and builds his personality structure on false premises. Even Hitler concedes that this finding is true, for he says in MEIN KAMPF:

> "There is a boy, let us say, of three. This is the age at which a child becomes conscious of his first impressions. In many intelligent people, traces of these early memories are found even in old age."

Under these circumstances, it will be well for us to inquire into the nature of Hitier's earliest environment and the impressions which he probably formed during this period. Our factual information on this phase of his life is practically nil. In MEIN KAMPF Hitler tries to create the impression that his home was rather peaceful and quiet, his "father a faithful civil servant, the mother devoting herself to the cares of the household and looking after her children with eternally the same loving care." It would seem that if this is a true representation of the home environment there would be no reason for his concealing it so scrupulously.

This is the only passage in a book of a thousand pages in which he even intimates that there were other children for his mother to take care of. No brother and no sister are mentioned in any other connection and even to his associate he has never admitted that there were other chidren besides his half-sister, Angela. Very little more is said about his mother, either in writing or speaking. This concealment in itself would make us suspicious about the truth of the statement quoted above. We become even more suspicious when we find that not a single patient manifesting Hitler's character traits has grown up in such a well-ordered and peaceful home environment.

If we read on in MEIN KAMPF we find that Hitler gives us a description of a child's life in a lower-class family. He says:

> "Among the five children there is a boy, let us say, of three... When the parents fight almost daily, their brutality leaves nothing to the imagination; then the results of such visual education must slowly but inevitably become apparent to the little one. Those who are not familiar with such conditions can hardly imagine the results, especially when the mutual differences express themselves in the form of brutal attacks on the part of the father towards the mother or to assaults due to drunkenness. The poor little boy at the age of six, senses things which would make even a grown-up person shudder. The other things the little fellow hears at home do not tend to further his respect for his surroundings."

In view of the fact that we now know that where were five children in the Hitler home and that his father liked to spend his spare time in the village tavern where he sometimes drank so heavily that he had to be brought horn by his wife or children, we begin to suspect that in this passage Hitler is, in all probability, describing conditions in his own home as a child.

If we accept the hypothesis that Hitler is actually talking about his own home when he describes conditions in the average lower-class family, we can obtain further information concerning the nature of his home environment. We read:

> "...things end badly indeed when the man from the very start goes his own way and the wife, for the sake of the children stands up against him. Quarreling and nagging set in, and in the same measure in which the husband becomes estranged from his wife, he becomes familiar with alcohol.....When he finally comes home... drunk and brutal, but always without a last cent or penny, then God have mercy on the scenes which follow. I witnessed all of this personally in hundreds of scenes and at the beginning with both disgust and indignation." (MK, 38)

When we remember the few friends that Hitler has made in the course of his life, and not a single intimate friend, one wonders where he had the opportunity of observing these scenes personally, hundreds of times, if it was not in his own home. And then he continues:

> "The other things the little fellow hears at home do not tend to further his respect for his surroundings. Not a single good shred is left for humanity, not a single institution is left unattacked; starting with the teacher, up to the head of the State, be it religion, or morality as such, be it the State or society, no matter which, everything is pulled down in the nastiest manner into the filth of a depraved mentality." (MK, 43)

All of this agrees with information obtained from other

sources whose veracity might otherwise be open to question. With this as corroborating evidence, however, it seems safe to assume that the above passages are a fairly accurate picture of the Hitler household and we may surmise that these scenes did arouse disgust and indignation in him at a very early age.

These feelings were aggravated by the fact that when his father was sober he tried to create an entirely different impression. At such times he stood very much on his dignity and prided himself on his position in the civil serviceo Even after he had retired from this service he always insisted on wearing his uniform when he appeared in public. He was scrupulous about his appearance and strode down the viliage street in his most dignified manner. When he spoke to his neighbors or acquaintances he did so in a very condescending manner and always demanded that they use his full title when they addressed him. If one of them happened to omit a part of it, he would call attention to their omission. He carried this to the point where, so informants tell us, he became a source of amusement to the other villagers and their children. At home, he demanded that the children address him as Herr Vater instead of using one of the intimate abbreviations or nicknames that children commonly do.

Father's lnfluence on Hitler's character.

We know from our study of many cases that the character of father is one of the major factors determining the character of the child during infancy, particularly that of a boy. In cases in which the father is a fairly well-integrated individual and presents a consistent pattern of behavior which the small boy can respect, he becomes a model which the child strives to emulate. The image the child has of his father becomes the cornerstone of his later character-structure and with its help he is able to integrate his own behavior along socially accepted lines. The importance of this first step in character development can scarcely be over-estimated. It is almost a prerequisite for a stable, secure and well-integrated personality in later life.

In Hitler's case, as in almost all other neurotics of his type, this step was not feasible. Instead of presenting an image of a consistent, harmonious, socially-adjusted and admirable individual which the child can use as a guide and model, the father shows himself to be a mass of contradictions. At times he plays the role of "a faithful civil servant" who respects his position and the society he serves, and demands that all others do likewise. At such times he is the soul of dignity, propriety, sternness and justice. To the outside world he tries to appear as a pillar of society whom all should respect and obey. At home, on the other hand, particularly after he had been drinking, he appears the exact opposite. He is brutal, unjust and inconsiderate. He has no respect for anybody or anything. The world is all wrong and an unfit place in which to live. At such times he also plays the part of the bully and whips his wife and children who are unable to defend themselves. Even the dog comes in for his share of his sadistic display.

Under such circumstances the child becomes confused and is unable to identify himself with a clear-cut pattern which he can use as a guide for his own adjustment. Not only is this a severe handicap in itself but in addition the child is given a distorted picture of the world around him and the nature of the people in it. The home, during these years, is his world and he judges the outside world in terms of it. The result is that the whole world appears as extremely dangerous, uncertain and unjust as a place in which to live and the child's impulse is to avoid it as far as possible because he feels unable to cope with it. He feels insecure, particularly since he can never predict beforehand how his father will behave when he comes home in the evening or what to expect from him. The person who should give him love, support and a feeling of security now fills him with anxiety, uneasiness and uncertainty.

His search for a competent guide.

As a child Hitler must have felt this lack very keenly for throughout his later life we find him searching for a strong masculine figure whom he can respect and emulate. The men with whom he had contact during his childhood evidently could not fill the role of guide to his complete satisfaction. There is some evidence that he attempted to regard some of his teachers in this way but whether it was the influence of his father's ranting or shortcomings in the teachers themselves, his attempts always miscarried. Later he attempted to find great men in history who could fill this need. Caesar, Napoleon and Frederick the Great are only a few of the many to whom he became attached. Although such, historic figures serve important role of this kind in the life of almost every child, they are in themselves inadequate. Unless a fairly solid foundation already exists in the mind of the child these heroes never become flesh and blood people inasmuch as the relationship is one-sided and lacks reciprocation. The same is also true of the political figures with which Hitler sought to identify himself during the Vienna period. For a time Schoenerer and Lueger became his heroes and although they were instrumental in forming some of his political beliefs and channeling his feelings, they were still too far removed from him to play the role of permanent guides and models.

During his career in the army we have an excellent example of Hitler's willingness to submit to the leadership of strong males who were willing to guide him and protect him. Throughout his army life there is not a shred of evidence to show that Hitler was anything but the model soldier as far as submissivehess and obedience are concerned. From a psychological point of view his life in the army was a kind of substitute for the home life he had always wanted but could never find, and he fulfilled his duties willingly and faithfully. He liked it so well that after he was wounded, in 1916, he wrote to his commanding officer and requested that he be called back to front duty before his leave had expired.

After the close of the war he stayed in the army and continued to be docile to his officers. He was willing to do anything they asked, even to the point of spying on his own comrades and then condemning them to death. When his officers singled him out to do special propaganda work because they believed he had a talent for speaking, he was overjoyed. This was the beginning of his political career, and here too we can find many manifestations of his search for a leader. In the beginning he may well have thought of himself as the "drummer-boy" who was heralding the coming of the great leader. Certain it is that during the early years of his career he was very submissive to a succession of important men to whom he looked for guidance - von Kahr, Ludendorff and Hindenburg, to name only a few.

It is true that in the end he turned upon them one after another and treated them in a despicable fashion, but usually this change came after he discovered their personal shortcomings and inadequacies. As in many neurotic people of Hitler's type who have a deep craving for guidance from an older man, their requirements grow with the years. By the time they reach maturity they are looking for, and can only submit to, a person who is perfect in every respect -literally a super-man. The result is that they are always trying to come in contact with new persons of high status in the hope that each one, in turn, will prove to be the ideal.

No sooner do they discover a single weakness or shortcoming than they depose him from the pedestal on which they have placed him. They then treat their fallen heroes badly for having failed to live up to their expectations. And so Hitler has spent his life looking for a competent guide but always ends up with the discovery that the person he has chosen falls short of his requirements and is fundamentally no more capable than himself. That this tendency is a carry-over from his early childhood is evidenced by the fact that throughout these years he always laid great stress on addressing these persons by their full titles. Shades of his father's training during his early childhood!

It may be of interest to note at this time that of all the titles that Hitler might have chosen for himself he is content with the simple one of "Fuehrer". To him this title is the greatest of them all. He has spent his life searching for a person worthy of the role but was unable to find one until he discovered himself. His goal is now to fulfill this role to millions of other people in a way in which he had hoped some person might do for him. The fact that the German people have submitted so readily to his leadership would indicate that a great many Germans were in a similar state of mind as Hitler himself and were not only willing, but anxious, to submit to anybody who could prove to them that he was competent to fill the role. There is some sociological evidence that this is probably so and that its origins lie in the structure of the German family and the dual role played by the father within the home as contrasted with the outside world. The duality, on the average is, of course, not nearly as marked as we have shown it to be in Hitler's case, but it may be this very fact which qualified him to identify the need and express it in terms which the others could understand and accept.

There is evidence that the only person in the world at the present time who might challenge Hitler in the role of leader is Roosevelt. Informants are agreed that he fears neither Churchill nor Stalin. He feels that they are sufficiently like himself so th at he can understand their psychology and defeat them at the game. Roosevelt, however, seems to be an enigma him. How a man can lead a nation of 150,000,000 people and keep them in line without a great deal of name-calling, shouting, abusing and threatening is a mystery to him. He is unable to understand how a man can be the leader of a large group and still act like a gentleman. The result is that he secretly admires Roosevelt to a considerable degree, regardless of what he publicly says about him.

Underneath he probably fears him inasmuch as he is unable to predict his actions.

Hitler's mother and her influence.

Hitler's father, however, was only a part of his early environment. There was also his mother who, from all reports, was a very decent type of woman. Hitler has written very little and said nothing about her publicly. Informants tell us, however, that she was an extremely conscientitious and hard-working individual whose life centered around her home and children. She was an exemplary housekeeper and there was never a spot or speck of dust to be found in the house - everything was very neat and orderly. She was a very devout Catholic and the trials and tribulations that fell upon her home she accepted with Christian resignation. Even her last illness, which extended over many months and caused her great pain, she endured without a single complaint. We may assume that she had to put up with much from her irrascible husband and it may be that at at times she did have to stand up against him for the welfare of her children. But all of this she probably accepted in the same spirit of abnegation. To her own children she was always extremely affectionate and generous although there is some reason to suppose that she was mean at times to her two step-children.

In any event, every scrap of evidence indicates that there was an extremely strong attachment between herself and Adolph. As previously pointed out, this was due in part to the fact that she had lost two, or possibly three, children before Adolph was born. Since he, too, was frail as a child it is natural that a woman of her type should do everything within her power to guard against another recurrence of her earlier experiences. The result was that she catered to his whims, even to the point of spoiling him, and that she was over-protective in her attitude towards him. We may assume that during the first five-years of Adolph's life, he was the apple of his mother's eye and that she lavished affection on him. In view of her husband's conduct and the fact that he was twenty-three years her senior and far from having a loving disposition, we may suppose that much of the affection that normally would have gone to him also found its way to Adolph.

The result was a strong libidinal attachment between mother and son. It is almost certain that Adolph had temper tantrums during this time but that these were not of a serious nature. Their immediatel purpose was to get his own way with his mother and he undoubtedly succeeded in achieving this end. They were a technique by which he could dominate her whenever he wished, either out of fear that she would lose his love or out of fear that if he continued he might become like his father. There is reason to suppose that she frequently condoned behavior of which the father would have disapproved and may have become a partner in forbidden activities during the father's absence. Life with his mother during these early years must have been a veritable paradise for Adolph except for the fact that his father would intrude and disrupt the happy relationship. Even when his father did not make a scene or lift his whip, he would demand attention from his wife which prevented her participation in pleasurable activities.

It was natural, under these circumstances, that Adolph should resent the intrusion into his Paradise and this undoubtedly aggravated the feelings of uncertainty and fear which his father's conduct aroused in him.

As he became older and the libidinal attachment to his mother became stronger, both the resentment and fear undoubtedly increased. Infantile sexual feelings were probably quite prominent in this relationship as well as fantasies of a childish nature. This is the Oedipus complex mentioned by psychologists and psychiatrists who have written about Hitler's personality. The great amount of affection lavished upon him by his mother and the undesirable character of his father served to develop this complex to an extraordinary degree. The more he hated his father the more dependent he became upon the affection and love of his mother, and the more he loved his mother the more afraid he became of his father's vengeance should his secret be discovered. Under these circumstances, little boys frequently fantasy about ways and means of ridding the environment of the intruder. There is reason to suppose that this also happened in Hitler's early life.

Influences determining his attitude towards love, women, marriage.

Two other factors entered into the situation which served to accentuate the conflict still further. One of these was the birth of a baby brother when he was five years of age. This introduced a new rival onto the scene and undoubtedly deprived him of some of his mother's affection and attention, particularly since the new child was also rather sickly. We may suppose that the newcomer in the family also became the victim of Adolph's animosity and that he fantasied about getting rid of him as he had earlier contemplated getting rid of his father. There is nothing abnormal in this except the intensity of the emotions involved.

The other factor which served to intensify these feelings was the fact that as a child he must have discovered his parents during intercourse. An examination of the data makes this conclusion most inescapable and from our knowledge of his father's character and past history it is not at all improbable. It would seem that his feelings on this occasion were very mixed. On the one hand, he was indignant at his father for what he considered to be a brutal assault upon his mother. On the other hand, he was indignant with his mother because she submitted so willingly to the father, and he was indignant with himself because he was powerless to intervene. Later, as we shall see, there was an hysterical re-living of this experience which played an important part in shaping his future destinies.

Being a spectator to this early scene had many repercussions. One of the most important of these was the fact that he felt that his mother had betrayed him in submitting to his father, a feeling which became accentuated still further when his baby brother was born. He lost much of his respect for the female sex and while in Vienna, Hanisch reports, he frequently spoke at length on the topic of love and marriage and that "he had very austere ideas about relations between men and women". Even at that time he maintained that if men only wanted to they could adopt a strictly moral way of living. "He often said it was the woman's fault if a man went astray" and "He used to lecture us about this, saying every woman can be had." In other words, he regarded woman as the seducer and responsible for man's downfall and he condemned them for their disloyalty.

These attitudes are probably the outcome of his early experiences with his mother who first seduced him into a love relationship and then betrayed him by giving herself to his father. Nevertheless, he still continued to believe in an idealistic form of love and marriage which would be possible if a loyal woman could be found. As we know, Hitler never gave himself into the hands of a woman again with the possible exception of his niece, Geli Raubal, which also ended in disaster. Outside of that single exception he has lived a loveless life. His distrust of both men and women is so deep that in all his history there is no record of a really intimate and lasting friendship.

The outcome of these early experiences was probably a feeling of being very much alone in a hostile world. He hated his father, distrusted his mother, and despised himself for his weakness. The immature child finds such a state of mind almost unendurable for any length of time and in order to gain peace and security in his environmlnt these feelings are gradually repressed from his memory.

This is a normal procedure which happens in the case of

every child at a relatively early age. This process of repression enables the child to reestablish a more or less friendly relationship with his parents without the interference of disturbing memories and emotions. The early conflicts, however, are not solved or destroyed by such a process and we must expect to find manifestations of them later on. When the early repression has been fairly adequate these conflicts lie dormant until adolescence when, due to the process of maturation, they are reawakened. In some cases they reappear in very much their original form, while in others they are expressed in a camouflaged or symbolic form.

In Hitler's case, however, the conflicting emotions and sentiments were so strong that they could not be held a latent state during this time. Quite early in his school career we find his conflicts appearing again in a symbolic form. Unfortunately, the symbols he unconsciously chose to express his own inner conflicts were such that they have seriously affected the future of the world. And yet these symbols fit his peculiar situation so perfectly that it was almost inevitable that they would be chosen as vehicles of expression.

Hitler
Psychological Analysis & Reconstruction

Part II

His early conflicts expressed in symbolic form.

Unconsciously, all the emotions he had once felt for his mother became transferred to Germany. This transfer of affect was relatively easy inasmuch as Germany, like his mother, was young and vigorous and held promise of a great future under suitable circumstances. Furthermore, he felt shut off from Germany as he now felt shut off from his mother, even though he secretly wished to be with her. Germany became a symbol of his ideal mother and his sentiments are clearly expressed in his writings and speeches. A few excerpts will serve to illustrate the transfer of emotion:

"The longing grew stronger to go there (Germany) where since my early youth I had been drawn by secret wishes and secret love."

"What I first had looked upon as an impassable chasm now spurred me on to greater love for my country than ever before."

"An unnatural separation from the great common Motherland."

"I appeal to those who, severed from the Motherland, ...and who now in painful emotion long for the hour that will allow them to return to the arms of the beloved mother."

It is significant that although Germans, as a whole, invariably refer to Germany as the "Fatherland", Hitler almost always refers to it as the "Motherland.

Just as Germany was ideally suited to symbolize his mother, so was Austria ideally suited to symbolize his father. Like his father, Austria was old, exhausted and decaying from within. He therefore transferred all his unconscious hatred from his father to the Austrian state. He could now give vent to all his pent-up emotions without exposing himself to the dangers he believed he would have encountered had he expressed these same feelings towards the persons really involved. In MEIN KAMPF he frequently refers to the Austrian state, for example, in terms such as these:

> "... an intense love for my native German-Austrian country and a bitter hatred against the Austrian state."

> "With proud admiration I compared the rise of the Reich with the decline of the Austrian state."

The alliance between Austria and Germany served to symbolize the marriage of his mother and father. Over and over again we find references to this alliance and we can see clearly how deeply he resented the marriage of his parents because he felt that his father was a detriment to his mother and only through the death of the former could the latter obtain her freedom and find her salvation. A few quotations will illustrate his sentiments:

> "And who could keep faith with an imperial dynasty which betrayed the cause of the German people for its own ignominious ends, a betrayal that occurred again and again."

> "What grieved us most was the fact that the whole system, was morally protected by the alliance with Germany, and thus Germaey herself...walked by the side of the corpse."

"...It suffices to state here that from my earliest youth I came to a conviction which never deserted me, but on the contrary grew stronger and stronger: that the protection of the German race presumed the destruction of Austria...that, above all else, the Royal House of Hapsburg was destined to bring misfortune upon the German nation."

"Since my heart had never beaten for an Austrian monarchy but only for a German Reich, I could only look upon the hour of the ruin of this state as the beginning of the salvation of the German nation."

When we have grasped the significance of this transference of affect we have made a long step in the direction of understanding Hitler's actions. Unconsciously he is not dealing with nations composed of millions of individuals but is trying to solve his personal conflicts and rectify the injustices of his childhood. Unable to enter into a "give-and-take" relationship with other human beings which might afford him an opportunity of resolving his conflicts in a realistic manner, he projects his personal problems on great nations and then tries to solve them on this unrealistic level. His microcosm has been inflated into a macrocosm.

We can now understand why Hitler fell on his knees and thanked God when the last war broke out. To him it did not mean simply a war, as such, but an opportunity of fighting for his symbolic mother - of proving his manhood and of being accepted by her. It was inevitable that he would seek enlistment in the German Army rather than in the Austrian Army and it was also inevitable, under these circumstances, that he would be a good and obedient soldier. Unconsciously it was as though he were a little boy who was playing the part of a man while his mother stood by and watched him. Her future welfare was his great concern and in order to prove his love he was willing, if need be, to sacrifice his own life for her.

The effects of Germany's defeat.

Everything went smoothly as long as he felt sure that all would turn out well in the end. He never complained about the hardships that were imposed on him and he never grumbled with the other men. He was happy in what he was doing and met the trials and tribulations of army life with his chin up until he discovered that things were going badly and that his symbolic mother was about to be degraded as he had imagined his real mother had been degraded in his childhood. To him it was as if his mother was again the victim of a sexual assault. This time it was the November Criminals and the Jews who were guilty of the foul deed and he promptly transferred his repressed hate to these new perpetrators.

When he became fully aware of Germany's defeat he reacted in a typically hysterical manner. He refused to accept or adjust to the situation on a reality level. Instead, he reacted to this event as he probably reacted to the discovery of his parents in intercourse. He writes:

> "I stumbled and tottered rearwards with burning eyes...Already a few hours later the eyes had turned into burning coals; it had become dark around me."

In another place he writes:

> "While everything began to go black again before my eyes, stumbling, I groped my way back to the dormitory, threw myself on my cot and buried my burning head in the covers and pillows."

At the time this happened he had been exposed to a slight attack of mustard gas. He immediately believed that he was blinded and speechless. Although he spent several weeks in hospital, neither his symptoms nor the development of the illness corresponded to those found in genuine gas cases. It has been definitely established that both the blindness and the mutism were of an hysterical nature. The physician who treated him at that time found his case so typical of hysterical symptoms in general that for years after the war he used it as an illustration in his courses given at a prominent German medical school. We know from a great many other cases that during the onset of such attacks the patient behaves in exactly the same manner as he did earlier in his life when confronted by a situation with the same emotional content. It is as though the individual were actually reliving the earlier experience over again. In Hitler's case this earlier experience was almost certainly the discovery of his parents in intercourse and that he interpreted this as a brutal assault in which he was powerless. He refused to believe what his eyes told him and the experience left him speechless.

That this interpretation is correct is evidenced by his imagery in dealing with the event later on. Over and over again we find figures of speech such as these:

> "...by what wiles the soul of the German has been raped."

> "...our German pacifists will pass over in silence the most bloody rape of the nation."

which illustrate his sentiments very clearly.

The origins of his belief in his mission and his longing for immortality.

It was while he was in the hospital suffering from hysterical blindness and mutism that he had the vision that he would liberate the Germans from their bondage and make Germany great. It was this vision that set him on his present political career and which has had such a determining influence on the course of world events. More than anything else it was this vision that convinced him that he was chosen by Providence and that he had a great mission to perform. This is probably the most outstanding characteristic of Hitler's mature personality and it is this which guides him with the "precision of a sleepwalker."

From an analysis of many other cases we know that such convictions never result from an adult experience alone. In order to carry conviction they must reawaken earlier beliefs which have their roots far back in childhood. It is, of course, nothing unusual for a child to believe that he is some special creation and destined to do great things before he dies. One can almost say that every child passes through such a period on his way to growing up. In many people remnants of such early beliefs are observable inasmuch as they feel or believe that Fate or Luck or Providence or some extra-natural power has chosen them for special favors. In most of these cases, however, the adult individual only half believes that this is really so even when a whole series of favorable events may make the hypothesis plausible. Only rarely do we find a firm conviction of this kind in adulthood and then only when there were extenuating circumstances in childhood which made such a belief necessary and convincing.

In Hitler's case the extenuating circumstances are relatively clear. Mention has already been made of the fact that his mother had given birth to at least two and possibly three children, all of whom had died prior to his own birth. He, himself, was a frail and rather sickly infant. Under these circumstances, his mother undoubtedly exerted herself to the utmost to keep him alive. He was unquestionably spoiled during this period and his survival was probably the great concern of the family as well as of the neighbors. From his earliest days there was, no doubt, considerable talk in the household about the death of the other children and constant comparisons between their progress and his own.

Children first become aware of death as a phenomenon very early in life and in view of these unusual circumstances it may have dawned on Hitler even earlier than with most children. The thought of death, in itself, is inconceivable to a small child and they usually are able to form only the vaguest conception of what it means or implies before they push it out of their minds, for later consideration. In Hitler's case, however, it was a living issue and the fears of the mother were in all likelihood communicated to him. As he pondered the problem in his immature way, he probably wondered why the others died while he continued to live. The natural conclusion for a child to draw would be that he was favored in some way or that he was chosen to live for some particular purpose. The belief that he was the "chosen one" would have been reinforced by the fact that as far as his mother was concerned he was very much the chosen one in comparison with her two step-children who were also living in the home at that time.

This belief must have been strengthened considerably when, at the age of five, his baby brother was born. This baby brother has undoubtedly played a much more important role in Adolph's life than has been acknowledged by his biographers. The pertinent fact at the moment, however, is that this brother too died before he was six years old. It was Adolph's first real experience with death and it must have brought up the problem of death again in a much more vivid form. Again, we can surmise, he asked himself why they died while he continues to be saved. The only plausible answer to a child at that age would be that he must be under divine protection. This may seem far-fetched and yet, as an adult, Hitler tells us that he felt exactly this way when he was at the front during the war, even before he had the vision.

Then, too, he speculated on why it is that comrades all around him are killed while he is saved and again he comes to the conclusion that Providence must be protecting him. Perhaps the exemplary courage he displayed in carrying messages at the front was due to the feeling that some kindly Fate was watching over him. Throughout MEIN KAMPF we find this type of thinking. It was Fate that had him born so close to the German border; it was Fate that sent him to Vienna to suffer with the masses; it was

Fate that caused him to do many things. The experience he reports at the front, when a voice told him to pick up his plate and move to another section of the trench just in time to escape a shell which killed all his comrades, must certainly have strengthened this belief to a marked degree and paved the way for his vision later on.

The Messiah. complex.

Another influence may have helped to solidify this system of belief. Among patients we very frequently find that children who are spoiled at an early age and establish a strong bond with their mother tend to question their paternity. Eldest children in particular are prone to such doubts and it is most marked in cases where the father is much older than the mother. In Hitler's case the father was twenty-three years older, or almost twice the age of the mother. Just why this should be is not clear, from a psychological point of view, but in such cases there is a strong tendency to believe that their father is not their real father and to ascribe their birth to some kind of supernatural conception. Usually such beliefs are dropped as the child grows older. It can be observed in young children, however, and can often be recovered in adults under suitable conditions. Due to the unsympathetic and brutal nature of his father we may suppose that there was an added incentive in rejecting him as his real father and postulating some other origin to himself.

The problem is not important in itself at the moment except insofar as it may help to throw some light on the origins of Hitler's conviction in his mission and his belief that he is guided by some extra-natural power which communicates to him what he should and should not do under varying circumstances. This hypothesis is tenable in view of the fact that during his stay in Vienna, when still in his early twenties, he grew a beard and again directly after the war when he again grew a Christ-like beard. Then, too, when he was a student at the Benedictine school his ambition was to join the Church and become an abbot or priest. All of these give some indication of a Messiah complex long before he had started on his meteoric career and become an open competitor of Christ for the affections of the German people.

Fear of death and desire for immortality.

Although beliefs of this kind are common during childhood they are usually dropped or are modified as the individual becomes older and more experienced. In Hitler's case, however, the reverse has taken place. The conviction became stronger as he grew older until, at the present time, it is the core of his thinking. Under these circumstances, we must suppose that some powerful psychological stream continued to nourish these infantile modes of thought. This psychological stream is probably, as it is in many other cases, a fear of death. It seems logical to suppose that in the course of his early deliberations on the deaths of his brothers his first conclusion was probably that all the others die and that consequently he too would die. His fear would not be allayed by his mother's constant concern over his well-being, which he may have interpreted as an indication that the danger was imminent. Such a conclusion would certainly be a valid one for a child to make under the circumstances.

The thought of his own death, however, is almost unbearable to a small child. Nothing is quite so demoralizing as the constant dread of self-annihilation. It gnaws away day and night and prevents him from enjoying the good things that life affords.

To rid himself of this devastating fear becomes his major objective. This is not easily accomplished, especially when all available evidence seems to corroborate the validity of the fear. In order to offset its potency he is almost driven to deny its reality by adopting the belief that he is of divine origin and that Providence

155

is protecting him from all harm. Only by use of such a technique is the child able to convince himself that, he will not die. We must also remember that in Hitler's case there was not only the unusual succession of deaths of siblings, but there was also the constant menace of his father's brutality which helped make the fear more intense than in most children. This danger could easily be exaggerated in Hitler's mind due to a sense of guilt concerning his feelings towards his respective parents and what his father might do to him if he discovered his secret. These feelings would tend to increase his fear of death at the same time that they caused him to reject his father. Both tendencies would serve to nourish the belief that he was of divine origin and was under its protection.

It is my belief that this basic fear of death is still present and active in Hitler's character at the present time. As time goes on and he approaches the age when he might reasonably expect to die, this infantile fear asserts itself more strongly. As a mature, intelligent man he knows that the law of nature is such that his physical self is destined to die. He is still not able, however, to accept the fact that he as an individual, his psyche, will also die. It is this element in his psychological structure which demands that he become immortal. Most people are able to take the sting out of this fear of death through religious beliefs in life after death, or through the feeling that a part of them, at least, will continue to go on living in their children. In Hitler's, case, both of these normal channels have been closed and he has been forced to seek immortality in a more direct form. He must arrange to go on living in the German people for at least a thousand years to come. In order to do this, he must oust Christ as a competitor and usurp his place in the lives of the German people.

In addition to evidence drawn from experience with patients which would make this hypothesis tenable, we have the evidence afforded by Hitler's own fears and attitudes. We have discussed these in detail in Section IV. Fear of assassination, fear of poisoning, fear of premature death, etc., all deal with the problem of death in an uncamouflaged form. One can, of course, maintain that in view or his position all these fears are more or less justified. There is certainly some truth in this contention but we also notice that as time goes on these fears have increased considerably until now they have reached the point where the precautions for his own safety far exceed those of any of his predecessors. As long as he could hold a plebescite every now and then and reassure himself that the German people loved him and wanted him, he felt better. Now that this is no longer possible, he has no easy way of curbing the fear and his uncertainty in the future becomes greater. There can be little doubt concerning his faith in the results of the plebescites. He was firmly convinced that the 98% vote, approving his actions, really represented the true feelings of the German people. He believed this because he needed such reassurance from time to time in order to carry on with a fairly easy mind and maintain his delusions.

When we turn to his fear of cancer we find no justification whatever for his belief, especially in view of the fact that several outstanding specialists in this disease have assured him that it is without foundation. Nevertheless, it is one of his oldest fears and he continues to adhere to it in spite of all the expert testimony to the contrary. This fear becomes intelligible when we remember that his mother died following an operation for cancer of the breast. In connection with his fear of death we must not forget his terrifying nightmares from which he awakes in a cold sweat and acts as though he were being suffocated. If our hypothesis is correct, namely, that a fear of death is one of the powerful unconscious streams which drive Hitler on in his mad career, then we can expect that as the war progresses and as he becomes older the fear will continue to increase. With the progress of events along their present course, it will be more and more difficult for him to feel that his mission is fulfilled and that he has successfully cheated death and achieved immortality in the German people. Nevertheless, we can expect him to keep on trying to the best of his ability as long as a ray of hope remains. The great danger is that if he feels that he cannot achieve immortality as the Great Redeemer he may seek it as the Great Destroyer who will live on in the minds of the German people for a thousand years to come. He intimated this in a conversation with Rauschning when he said:

> "We shall not capitulate -- no, never. We may be destroyed, but if we are, we shall drag a world with us--a world in flames."

With him, as with many others of his type, it may well be a case of immortality of any kind at any price.

Sexual development.

Closely interwoven with several of the themes which have already been elaborated is the development of his sexual life. From what we know about his mother's excessive cleanliness and tidiness we may assume that she employed rather stringent measures during the toilet training period of her children. This usually results in a residual tension in this area and is regarded by the child as a severe frustration which arouses feelings of hostility. This facilitates an alliance with his infantile aggression which finds an avenue for expression through anal activities and fantasies. These usually center around soiling, humiliation and destruction, and form the basis of a sadistic character.

Here, again, we may assume that the experience was more intense in Hitler's case than in the average due to the strong attachment and spoiling of his mother in early infancy. Unaccustomed to minor frustrations which most children must learn to endure, prior to the toilet training, he was poorly equipped to deal with this experience which plays an important role in the life of all infants. Even now, as an adult, we find Hitler unable to cope with frustrating experiences on a mature level. That a residual tension from this period still exists in Hitler is evidenced by the frequency of imagery in his speaking and writing which deal with dung and dirt and smell. A few illustrations may help to clarify his unconscious preoccupation with these subjects.

"You don't understand: we are just passing a magnet over a dunghill, and we shall see presently how much iron was in the dunghill and has clung to the magnet." (By 'dunghill' Hitler meant the German people.)

"And when he (the Jew) turns the treasures over in his hand they are transformed into dirt and dung."

"...Ones hands hands seize slimy jelly; it slips through one's fingers only to collect again in the next moment."

"Charity is sometimes actually comparable to the manure which is spread on the field, not out of love for the latter, but out of precaution for one's own benefit later on."

"...dragged into the dirt and filth of the lowest depths."

"Later the smell of these caftan wearers made me ill. Added to this were their dirty clothes and their none too heroic appearance."

"...The rottenness of artificially nurtured conditions of peace has more than once stunk to high heaven."

His libidinal development, however, was not arrested at this point but progressed to the genital level at which the Oedipus complex, already referred to, developed.

This complex, as we have seen, was aggravated by his mother's pregnancy at precisely the age when the complex normally reaches its greatest intensity. In addition to accentuating his hatred for his father and estranging him from his mother, we can assume that this event at this particular time served to generate an abnormal curiosity in him. He, like all children at this age, must have wondered how the unborn child got into the mother's stomach and how it was going to get out.

These three reactions have all played an important part in Hitler's psychosexual development. It would seem from the evidence that his aggressive fantasies towards the father reached such a point that he became afraid of the possibility of retaliation if his secret desires were discovered. The retaliation he probably feared was that his father would castrate him or injure his genital capacity in some way - a fear which is later expressed in substitute form in his syphilophobia. Throughout MEIN KAMPF he comes back to the topic of syphilis again and again and spends almost an entire chapter describing its horrors. In almost all cases we find that a fear of this sort is rooted in a fear of genital injury during childhood. In many cases this fear was so overpowering that the child abandoned his genital sexuality entirely and regressed to earlier stages of libidinal development. In order to maintain these repressions later in life he uses the horrors of syphilis as a justification for his unconscious fear that genital sexuality is dangerous for him, and also as a rationalization for his avoidance of situations in which his earlier desires might be aroused.

In abandoning the genital level of libidinal development the individual becomes impotent as far as heterosexual relations are concerned. It would appear, from the evidence, that some such process took place during Hitler's early childhood. Throughout his early adult life, in Vienna, in the Army, in Munich, in Landesberg, no informant has reported a heterosexual relationship. In fact, the informants of all these periods make a point of the fact that he had absolutely no interest in women or any contact with them. Since he has come to power his peculiar relationship to women has been so noticeable that many writers believe that he is asexual. Some have surmised that he suffered a genital injury during the last war, others that he is homosexual. The former hypothesis, for which there is not a shred of real evidence, is almost certainly false. The second hypothesis we will examine later on.

The diffusion of the sexual instinct.

When a regression of this kind take [error in original document] place the sexual instinct usually becomes diffuse and many organs which have yielded some sexual stimulation in the past become permanently invested with sexual significance. The eyes, for example, may become a substitute sexual organ and seeing then takes on a sexual significance. This seems to have happened in Hitler's case for a number of informants have commented on his delight in witnessing strip-tease and nude dancing numbers on the stage. On such occasions he can never see enough to satisfy him even though he uses opera glasses in order to observe more closely. Strip-tease artists are frequently invited to the Brown House, in Munich, to perform in private and there is evidence that he often invites girls to Berchtesgaden for the purpose of exhibiting their bodies. On his walls are numerous pictures of obscene nudes which conceal nothing and he takes particular delight in looking through a collection of pornographic pictures which Hoffmann has made for him. We also know the extreme pleasure he derives from huge pageants, circus performances, opera, and particularly the movies of which he can never get enough. He has told informants that he gave up flying not only because of the danger involved but because he could not see enough of the country. For this reason, automobile travel is his favorite form of transportation. From all of this it is evident that seeing has a special sexual significance for him. This probably accounts for his "hypnotic glance" which has been the subject of comment by so many writers.

Some have reported that at their first meeting Hitler fixated them with his eyes as if "to bore through them." It is also interesting that when the other person meets his stare, Hitler turns his eyes to the ceiling and keeps them there during the interview. Then, too, we must not forget that in the moment of crisis his hysterical attack manifested itself in blindness.

In addition to the eyes, the anal region has also become highly sexualised and both faeces and buttocks become sexual objects. Due to early toilet training, certain inhibitions have been set up which prevent their direct expression. However, we find so many instances of imagery of this kind, particularly in connection with sexual topics, that we must assume that this area has unusual sexual significance. The nature of this significance we will consider in a moment.

The mouth, too, seems to have become invested as an erogenous zone of great importance. Few authors or informants have neglected to mention Hitler's peculiar dietary habits. He consumes tremendous quantities of sweets, candies, cakes, whipped cream, etc., in the course of a day in addition to his vegetable diet. On the other hand, he refuses to eat meat, drink beer or smoke, all of which suggest certain unconscious inhibitions in this area. In addition, he has a pathological fear of poisoning by mouth, and has shown an obsessional preoccupation at times with mouth washing. These suggest a reaction formation or defense against an unacceptable tendency to take something into his mouth or get something out which from one point of view appears to be disgusting. In this connection we must not forget his resolve to starve himself to death after the failure of the Beer Hall Putsch, his hysterical mutism at the end of the last war, and his love of speaking. The significance of these we shall consider later on.

Disturbance of love relations.

The second effect of his mother's pregnancy was his

estrangement from her. The direct result of this was, on the one hand, an idealization of love but without a sexual component and, on the other hand, the setting up of a barrier against intimate relationships with other people, particularly women. Having been hurt once, he unconsciously guards himself against a similar hurt in the future. In his relationship to his niece, Geli, he tried to overcome this barrier but he was again disappointed and since then has not exposed himself to a really intimate relationship either with man or woman. He has cut himself off from the world in which love plays any part for fear of being hurt and what love he can experience is fixated on the abstract entity – Germany, which, as we have seen, is a symbol of his ideal mother. This is a love relationship in which sex plays no direct part.

Origin of his perversion.

The third outcome of his mother's pregnancy was to arouse an excessive curiosity. The great mystery to children of this age, who find themselves in this situation, is how the unborn child got into the mother's stomach and how it is going to get out. Even in cases where the children have witnessed parental intercourse, this event is rarely linked with the ensuing pregnancy. Since, in their limited experience, everything that gets into their stomach enters by way of the mouth and everything that comes out usually does so by way of the rectum, they are prone to believe that conception somehow takes place through the mouth and that the child will be born via the anus. Hitler, as a child, undoubtedly adhered to this belief but this did not satisfy his curiosity. He evidently wanted to see for himself how it came out and exactly what happened.

This curiosity laid the foundation for his strange perversion which brought all three of his sexualized zones into play. In her description of sexual experiences with Hitler, Geli stressed the fact that it was of the utmost importance to him that she squat over him in such a way that he could see everything. It is interesting, that Roehm, in an entirely different connection, once said:

> "He (Hitler) is thinking about the peasant girls. When they stand in the fields and bend down at their work so that you can see their behinds, that's what he likes, especially when they've got big round ones. That's Hitler's sex life. What a man."

Hitler, who was present, did not stir a muscle but only stared at Roehm with compressed lips.

Hitler
Psychological Analysis & Reconstruction
Part III

From a consideration of all the evidence it would seem that Hitler's perversion is as Geli has described it. The great danger in gratifying it, however, is that the individual might get faeces or urine into his mouth. It is this danger that must be guarded against.

Return to the womb.

Another possibility in infantile thinking presents itself in this connection. When the home environment is harsh and brutal, as it was in Hitler's case, the small child very frequently envies the position of passivity and security the unborn child enjoys within the mother. This, in turn, gives rise to fantasies of finding a way in to the longed for claustrum and ousting his rival in order that he may take his place. These fantasies are usually of very brief duration because, as the child believes, he would have nothing to eat or drink except faeces and urine. The thoughht of such a diet arouses feelings of disgust and consequently he abandons his fantasies in order to avoid these unpleasant feelings. In many psychotics, however, these fantasies continue and strive to express themselves overtly. The outstanding bit of evidence in Hitler's case that such fantasies were present is to be found in the Kehlstein or Eagle's Nest which he has built for himself near Berchtesgaden. Interestingly enough, many people have, commented that only a madman would conceive of such a place, let alone try to build it.

From a symbolic point of view one can easily imagine that this is a materialization of a child's conception of the return to the womb. First there is a long hard road, then a heavily guarded entrance, a trip through a long tunnel to an extremely inaccessible place. Then one can be alone, safe and undisturbed, and revel in the joys that Mother Nature bestows. It is also interesting to note that very few people have ever been invited there and many of Hitier's closest associates are either unaware of its existence or have only seen it from a distance. Extraordinarily enough, Francois-Poncet is one of the few people who was ever invited to visit there. In the French Yellow Book, he gives us an extremely vivid description of the place, a part of which may be worthwhile quoting:

> "The approach is by a winding road about nine miles long, boldly cut out of the rock... the road comes to an end in front of a long underground passage leading into the mountain, enclosed by a heavy double door of bronze. At the far end of the underground passage a wide lift, panelled with sheets of copper, awaits the visitor. Through a vertical shaft of 330 feet cut right through the rock, it rises up to the level of the Chancellor's dwelling place. Here is reached the astonishing climax. The visitor finds himself in a strong and massive building containing a gallery with Roman pillars, an immense circular hall with windows all around,... It gives the impression of being suspended in space, an almost overhanging wall of bare rock rises up abruptly. The whole,

bathed in the twilight of the autumn evening, is grandiose, wild, almost hallucinating. The visitor wonders whether he is awake or dreaming." (943)

If one were asked to plan something which represented a return to the womb, one could not possibly surpass the Kehlstein. It is also significant that Hitler often retires to this strange place to await instructions concerning the course he is to pursue.

Vegetarianism.

We can surmise from the psychological defenses Hitler has set up, that there was a period during which he struggled against these tendencies. In terms of unconscious symbolism meat is almost synonomous with faeces and beer with urine. The fact that there is a strict taboo on both would indicate that these desires are still present and that it is only by refraining from everything symbolizing them that he can avoid arousing anxieties. Rauschning reports that Hitler, following Wagner, attributed much of the decay of cur civilization to meat eating. That the decadence "had its origin in the abdomen -- chronic constipation, poisoning of the juices, and the results of drinking to excess." This assertion suggests decay (contamination, corruption, pollution, and death) as the resultant of constipation, that is, feaces in the gastro-intestinal tract, and if this is so, decay might be avoided both by not eating anything resembling feaces and by taking purges or ejecting as frequently as possible. It has been reported that Hitler once said that he was confident that all nations would arrive at the point where they would not feed any more on dead animals. It is interesting to note that according to one of our most reliable informants Hitler only became a real vegetarian after the death of his niece, Geli. In clinical practice, one almost invariably finds compulsive vegetarianism setting in after the death of a loved object.

We may, therefore, regard Hitler's perversion as a compromise between psychotic tendencies to eat faeces and drink urine on the one hand, and to live a normal socially adjusted life on the other. The compromise is not, however, satisfactory to either side of his nature and the struggle between these two diverse tendencies continues to rage unconsciously. We must not suppose that Hitler gratifies his strange perversion frequently. Patients of this type rarely do and in Hitler's case it is highly probable that he has permitted himself to go this far only with his niece, Geli. The practice of this perversion represents the lowest depths of degradation.

Masochistic gratifications.

In most patients suffering from this perversion the unconscious forces only get out of control to this degree when a fairly strong love relationship is established and sexuality makes decisive demands. In other cases where the love component is less strong the individual contents himself with less degrading activities. This is brought out cleariy in the case of Rene Mueller who confided to her director, Zeissler (921), who had asked her what was troubling her after spending an evening at the Chancelllory, "that the evening before she had been with Hitler and that she had been sure that he was going to have intercourse with her; that they had both undressed and were apparently getting ready for bed when Hitler fell on the floor and begged her to kick him. She demurred but he pleaded with her and condemned himself as unworthy, heaped all kinds of accusations on his own head and just grovelled around in an agonizing manner. The scene became intolerable to her and she finally acceded to his wishes and kicked him. This excited him greatly and he begged for more and more, always saying that it was even better than he deserved and that he was not worthy to be in the same room with her. As she continued to kick him he became more and more excited...." Rene Mueller committed suicide shortly after this experience. At this place it night be well to note that Eva Braun, his present female companion, has twice attempted suicide, Geli was either murdered or committed suicide and Unity Mitford has attempted suicide. Rather an unusual record for a man who has had so few affairs with women.

Hanfstaengl, Strasser, and Rauschning, as well as several other informants, have reported that even in company when Hitler is smitten with a girl, he tends to grovel at her feet in a most disgusting manner. Here, too, he insists on telling the girl that he is unworthy to kiss her hand or to sit near her and that he hopes she will be kind to him, etc. From all this we see the constant struggle against complete degradation whenever any affectionate components enter into the picture. It now becomes clear that the only way in which Hitler can control these copraphagic tendencies or their milder manifestations is to isolate himself from any intimate relationships in which warm feelings of affection or love might assert themselves. As soon as such feelings are aroused, he feels compelled to degrade himself in the eyes of the loved object and eat their dirt figuratively, if not literally. These tendencies disgust him just as much as they disgust us, but under these circumstances they get out of control and he despises himself and condemns himself for his weakness. Before considering futher the effects of this struggle on his manifest behavior, we must pause for a moment to pick up another thread.

Femininity.

We notice that in all of these activities Hitler plays the passive role. His behavior is masochistic in the extreme inasmuch as he derives sexual pleasure from punishment inflicted on his own body. There is every reason to suppose that during his early years, instead of identifying himself with his father as most boys do, he identified himself with his mother. This was perhaps easier for him than for most boys since, as we have seen, there is a large feminine component in his physical makeup. His mother, too, must have been an extremely masochistic individual or she never would have entered into this marriage nor would she have endured the brutal treatment from her husband. An emotional identification with his mother would, therefore, carry him in the direction of a passive, sentimental, abasive and submissive form of adjustment. Many writers and informants have commented on his feminine characteristics - his gait, his hands, his mannerisms and ways of thinking. Hanfstaengl reports that when he showed Dr. Jung a specimen of Hitler's handwriting, the latter immediately exclaimed that it was a typically feminine hand. His choice of art as a profession might also be interpreted as a manifestation of a basic feminine identification.

There are definite indications of such an emotional adjustment later in life. The outstanding of these is perhaps his behavior towards his officers during the last war. His comrades report that during the four years he was in service he was not only over-submissive to all his officers but frequently volunteered to do their washing and take care of their clothes. This would certainly indicate a strong tendency to assume the feminine role in the presence of a masculine figure whenever this was feasible and could be duly rationalized. His extreme sentimentality, his emotionality, his occasional softness and his weeping, even after he became Chancellor, may be regarded as manifestations of a fundamental feminine pattern which undoubtedly had its origins in his relationship to his mother. His persistent fear of cancer, which was the illness from which his mother died, may also be considered as an expression of his early identification with her.

Although we cannot enter into a discussion concerning the frequency of this phenomenon in Germany, it may be well to note that there is sociological evidence which would indicate that it is probably extremely common. If further research on the subject should corroborate this evidence, it might prove of extreme value to our psychological warfare program insofar as it would give us a key to the understanding of the basic nature of the German male character, and the role that the Nazi organization plays in their inner life.

Homosexuality.

The great difficulty is that this form of identification early in life carries the individual in the direction of passive homosexuality. Hitler has for years been suspected of being a homosexual, although there is no reliable evidence that he has actually engaged in a relationship of this kind. Rauschning reports that he has met two boys who claimed that they were Hitler's homosexual partners, but their testimony can scarcely be taken at its face value. More condemning would be the remarks dropped by Foerster, the Danzig Gauleiter, in conversations with Rauschning. Even here, however, the remarks deal only with Hitler's impotence as far as heterosexual relations go without actually implying that he indulges in homosexuality. It is probably true that Hitler calls Foerster "Bubi", which is a common nickname employed by homosexuals in addressing their partners. This alone, however, is not adequate proof that he has actually indulged in homosexual practices with Foerster, who is known to be a homosexual.

The belief that Hitler is homosexual has probably developed (a) from the fact that he does show so many feminine characteristics, and (b) from the fact that there were so many homosexuals in the Party during the early days and many continue to occupy important positions. It does seem that Hitler feels much more at ease with homosexuals than with normal persons, but this may be due to the fact that they are all fundamentally social outcasts and consequently have a community of interests which tends to make them think and feel more or less alike. In this connection it is interesting to note that homosexuals, too, frequently regard themselves as a special form of creation or as chosen ones whose destiny it is to initiate a new order.

The fact that underneath they feel themselves to be different and ostracized from normal social contacts usually makes them easy converts to a new social philosophy which does not discriminate against them. Being among civilization's discontents, they are always willing to take a chance of something new which holds any promise of improving their lot, even though their chances of success may be small and the risk great. Having little to lose to begin with, they can afford to take chances which others would refrain from taking. The early Nazi party certainly contained many members who could be regarded in this light. Even today Hitler derives pleasure from looking at men's bodies and associating with homosexuals. Strasser tells us that his personal body guard is almost always 100% homosexuals.

He also derives considerable pleasure from being with his Hitler Youth and his attitude towards them frequently tends to be more that of a woman than that of a man.

There is a possibility that Hitler has participated in a homosexual relationship at some time in his life. The evidence is such that we can only say there is a strong tendency in this direction which, in addition to the manifestations already enumerated, often finds expression in imagery concerning being attacked from behind or being stabbed in the back. His nightmares, which frequently deal with being attacked by a man and being suffocated, also suggest strong homosexual tendencies and a fear of them. From these indications, however, we would conclude that for the most part these tendencies have been repressed, which would speak against the probability of their being expressed in overt form. On the other hand, persons suffering from his perversion sometimes do indulge in homosexual practices in the hope that they might find sexual gratification. Even this perversion would be more acceptable to them than the one with which they are afflicted.

Early school years.

The foundations of all the diverse patterns we have been considering were laid during the first years of

Hitler's life. Many of them, as we have seen, were due primarily to the peculiar structure of the home, while others developed from constitutional factors or false interpretations of events.

Whatever their origins may have been, they did set up anti-social tendencies and tensions which disturbed the child to a high degree. From his earliest days it would seem he must have felt that the world was a pretty had place in which to live. To him it must have seemed as though the world was filled with insurmountable hazards and obstacles which prevented him from obtaining adequate gratifications, and dangers which would menace his well-being if he attempted to obtain them in a direct manner. The result was that an unusual amount of bitterness against the world and the people in it became generated for which he could find no suitable outlets. As a young child he must have been filled with feelings of inadequacy, anxiety and guilt which made him anything but a happy child.

It would seem, however, that he managed to repress most of his troublesome tendencies and make a temporary adjustment to a difficult environment before he was six years old, because at that time he entered school and for the next years he was an unusually good student. All of the report cards that have been found from the time he entered school until he was eleven years old, show an almost unbroken line of "A's" in all his school subjects. At the age of eleven the bottom dropped right out of his academic career. From an "A" student he suddenly dropped to a point where he failed in almost all his subjects and had to repeat the year. This amazing about-face only becomes intelligible when we realize that his baby brother died at that time. We can only surmise that this event served to reawaken his earlier conflicts and disrupt his psychological equilibrium.

In Hitler's case we may suppose that this event affected him in at least two important ways. First, it must have reawakened fears of his own death which, in turn, strengthened still further the conviction that he was the "chosen one" and under divine protection. Second, it would seem that he connected the death of his brother with his own thinking and wishing on the subject. Unquestionably, he hated this intruder and frequently thought of how nice it would be if he were removed from the scene. Unconsciously, if not consciously, he must have felt that the brother's death was the result of his own thinking on the subject. This accentuated his feelings of guilt on the one hand, while it strengthened still further his belief in special powers of Divine origin on the other. To think about these things was almost synonomous with having them come true. In order to avoid further guilt feelings he had to put a curb on his thinking processes. The result of this inhibition on thinking was that Hitler the good student was transformed into Hitler the poor student. Not only did he have to repeat the school year during which the brother died, but ever after his academic performance was mediocre, to say the least. When we examine his later report cards we find that he does well only in such subjects as drawing and gymnastics, which require no thinking. In all the other subjects such as mathematics, languages or history, which require some thinking, his work is on the borderline - sometimes satisfactory and sometimes unsatisfactory.

We can easily imagine that it was during this period that the father's ire was aroused and he began to bring pressure on the boy to apply himself in his school work and threatened dire consequences if he failed to do so. From sociological evidence it would seem that this is about the age at which most German fathers first take a real interest in their sons and their education. If Hitler's father followed this general pattern, we can assume that he had cause to be irate at his son's performance. The constant struggle between himself and his father, which he describes in MEIN KAMPF, is probably true although the motivations underlying his actions were in all likelihood quite different from those he describes. He was approaching the adolescent period and

173

this, together with his little brother's death, served to bring many dormant attitudes nearer the surface of consciousness.

Many of these attitudes now found expression in the father-son relationship. Briefly enumerated these would be (a) rejection of the father as a model; (b) an inhibition against following a career which demanded thinking; (c) the anal tendencies which found an outlet of expression in smearing; (d) his passive, feminine tendencies, and (e) his masochistic tendencies and his desire to be dominated by a strong masculine figure. He was not, however, ready for an open revolt for he tells us in his autobiography that he believed passive resistance and obstinacy were the best course and that if he followed them long enough, his father would eventually relent and allow him to leave school and follow an artist's career. As a matter of fact, his brother Alois, in 1930, before the Hitler myth was well established, reported, that his father never had any objection to Adolph's becoming an artist but that he did demand that Adolph do well in school. From this we might surmise that the friction between father and son was not determined so much by his choice of a career as by unconscious tendencies which were deriving satisfaction from the antagonism.

Later school career.

He carried the same pattern into the schools where he was forever antagonizing his teachers and the other boys. He has tried to create the impression that he was a leader among his classmates, which is most certainly false. More reliable evidence indicates that he was unpopular among his classmates as well as among his teachers who considered him lazy, uncooperative and a trouble-maker. The only teacher during these years with whom he was able to get along was Ludwig Poetsch, an ardent German Nationalist. It would he an error, however, to suppose that Poetsch inculcated these nationalist feelings in Hitler. It is much more logical to assume that all these feelings were present in Hitler before he came in contact with Poetsch and that his nationalist teachings only offered Hitler a new outlet for the expression of his repressed emotions. It was probably during this period that he discovered a resemblance between the young state of Germany and his mother, and between the old Austrian monarchy and his father. At this discovery he promptly joined the Nationalist group of students who were defying the authority of the Austrian state. In this way he was able to proclaim openly his love for his mother and advocate the death of his father. These were feelings he had had for a long time but was unable to express. Now he was able to obtain partial gratification through the use of symbols.

The death of his father.

This probably served to increase the friction between father and son, for in spite of what Hitler says the best evidence seems to indicate that the father was anti-German in his sentiments. This again placed father and son on opposite sides of the fence and gave them new cause for hostility. There is no telling how this would have worked out in the long run because while the struggle between the two was at its height, the father fell dead on the street. The repercussions of this event must have been severe and reinforced all those feelings which we have described in connection with the brother's death. Again, it must have seemed like a fulfillment of a wish and again there must have been severe feelings of guilt, with an additional inhibition on thinking processes.

His school work continued to decline and it seems that in order to avoid another complete failure, he was taken from the school at Linz and sent to school in Steyr. He managed to complete the year, however, with marks which were barely satisfactory. It was while he was there that the doctor told him that he had a disease from which he would never recover. His reaction to this was severe since it brought the possibility of his own death very much into the foreground and aggravated all his childhood fears. The result was that he did not return to school and finish his course, but stayed at home where he lived a life which was marked by passivity. He neither studied nor worked but spent most of his time in bed where he was again spoiled by his mother who catered to his every need despite her poor financial circumstances.

One could suppose that this was the materialization of his conception of Paradise inasmuch as it reinstated an earlier childhood situation which he had always longed for. It would seem from his own account, however, that things did not go too smoothly, for he writes in MEIN KAMPF:

> "When at the age of fourteen, the young man is dismissed from school, it is difficult to say which is worse; his unbelievable ignorance as far as knowledge and ability are concerned, or the biting impudence of his behavior combined with an immorality which makes one's hair stand on end...The three year old child has now become a youth of fifteen who despises all authority... now he loiters about, and God knows when he comes home."

We can imagine the deaths of his brother and his father in rapid succession had filled him with such guilt that he could not enjoy this idyllic situation to the full. Perhaps the situation aroused desires in him which he could no longer face on a conscious level and he could only keep these in check by either remaining in bed and playing the part of a helpless child or absenting himself from the situation entirely. In any case, he must have been a considerable problem to his mother who died four years after his father. Dr. Bloch informs us that her great concern in dying was: "What would become of poor Adolph, he is still so young." At this time Adolph was eighteen years of age. He had failed at school and had not gone to work. He describes himself at this time as a milk-sop, which he undoubtedly was.

Admission examinations to Academy of Art.

Two months before his mother's death he had gone to Vienna to take the entrance examinations for admission to the Academy of Art. At this time he knew that his mother was in a critical condition and that it was only a matter of a few months before death would overtake her. He knew, therefore, that this easy existence at home would shortly come to an end and that he would then have to face the cold, hard world on his own. It is sometimes extraordinary how events in the lifetime of an individual fall together. The first day's assignment on the examination was to draw a picture depicting "The Expulsion from Paradise". It must have seemed to him that Fate had chosen this topic to fit his personal situation. On the second day he must have felt that Fate was rubbing it in when he found the assignment to be a picture depicting "An Episode of the Great Flood". These particular topics in his situation met have aroused such intense emotional reactions within him that he could hardly be expected to do his best. Art critics seem to feel that he has some artistic talent even though it is not outstanding. The comment of the examiners was: "Too few heads." We can understand this in view of the circumstances under which he had taken the examination.

Death of his mother.

He returned home shortly after the examinations. He helped to look after his mother who was rapidly failing and in extreme pain. She died on December 21, 1907 and was buried on Christmas Eve. Adolph was completely broken and stood for a long time at her grave after the remainder of the family had left. Dr. Bloch says: "In all my career I have never seen anyone so prostrate with grief as Adolph Hitler." His world had come to an end. Not long after the funeral he left for Vienna in order to follow in his father's footsteps and make his own way in the world. He made a poor job of it, however. He could not hold a job when he had one, and sunk lower and lower in the social scale until he was compelled to live with the dregs of society.

Vienna days.

As he writes about these experiences in MEIN KAMPF one gets the impression that it was a terrific struggle against overwhelming odds. From what we now know of Adolph Hitler it would seem more likely that this existance yielded him considerable gratification in spite of its hardships. It is perfectly clear from what Hanisch writes that with a very small amount of effort he could have made a fair living and improved his condition by painting water-colors. He refused to make this effort and preferred to live in the filth and poverty which surrounded him. There must have been something in this that he liked, consciously or unconsciously.

When we examine Hanisch's book carefully, we find the answer. Hitler's life in Vienna was one of extreme passivity in which activity was held at the lowest level consistent with survival. He seemed to enjoy being dirty and even filthy in his appearance and personal cleanliness. This can mean only one thing, from a psychological point of view, namely that his perversion was in the process of maturation and was finding gratification in a more or less symbolic form. His attitude during this period could be summed up in the following terms: "I enjoy nothing more than to lie around while the world defacates on me." And he probably delighted in being covered with dirt, which was tangible proof of the fact. Even in these days he lived in a flophouse which was known to be inhabited by men who lent themselves to homosexual practices, and it was probably for this reason that he was listed on the Vienna police record as a "sexual pervert."

Nobody has ever offered an explanation of why he remained in Vienna for over five years if his life there was as distasteful and the city disgusted him to the degree that he claims in his autobiography. He was free to leave whenever he wished and could have gone to his beloved Germany years earlier if he had so desired. The fact of the matter is that he probably derived great masochistic satisfaction from his miserable life in Vienna, and it was not until his perversion became full-blown and he realized its implications that he fled to Munich at the beginning of 1913.

Anti-Semitism.

With the development of his perverse tendencies we also find the development of his anti-Semitism. There is absolutely no evidence that he had any anti-Semitic feeling before he left Linz or that he had any during the first years of his stay in Vienna. On the contrary, he was on the very best terms with Dr. Bloch while he was in Linz and sent him postcards with very warm sentiments for slome time after he went to Vienna. Furthermore, his closest friends in Vienna were Jews, some of whom were extremely kind to him. Then, too, we must remember that his godfather, who lived in Vienna, was a Jew and it is possible that during his first year there he might have lived with this family. Most of the records of his mother's death are incorrect and place the event exactly one year after it had happened. During this year Hitler lived in Vienna but we have no clue as to what he did or how he managed to live without money during this intervening year.

All we know is that he had time for painting during this period for he submitted the work he had done to the Academy of Art the following October. He was not admitted to the examination, however, because the examiners found the work of this period unsatisfactory. Shortly afterwards, he applied for admission to the School of Architecture but was rejected. The cause of his rejection was probably inadequate talent rather than the fact that he had not completed his course in the Realschule. It is only after this happened that we find him going to work as a laborer on a construction job, and from then on we have a fairly complete picture of his activities.

We know that he had very little money when he left Linz, certainly not enough to live on for almost an entire year while he spent his time in painting. Since the date of his mother's death has been so universally distorted, it would seem that efforts were being made to cover something which happened during this intervening year. My guess would be that he lived with his Jewish godparents who supported him while he was preparing work for the Academy. When he failed to be admitted at the end of a year, they put him out and made him go to work. There is one bit of evidence for this hypothesis. Hanisch, in his book, mentions in passing that when they were particularly destitute he went with Hitler to visit a well-to-do Jew whom Hitler said was his father. The wealthy Jew would have nothing to do with him and sent him on his way again. There is scarcely a possibility that Hitler's father was a Jew, but Hanisch might easily have understood him to say father when he said godfather. This would certainly make much more sense and would indicate that Hitler had contact with his godparents before the visit and that they were fed up with him and would help him no further.

Projection.

Hitler's outstanding defense mechanism is one commonly called PROJECTION. It is a technique by which the ego of an individual defends itself against unpleasant impulses, tendencies or characteristics by denying their existence in himself while he attributes them to others. Innumerable examples of this mechanism could be cited in Hitler's case, but a few will suffice for purposes of illustration:

> "In the last six years I had to stand intolerable things from states like Poland."

> "It must be possible that the German nation can live its life...without being constantly molested."

"Social democracy...directs a bombardment of lies and calumnies towards the adversary who seemed most dangerous, till finally the nerves of those who have been attacked give out and they for the sake of peace, bow down to the hated enemy."

"For this peace proposal of mine I was abused, and personally insulted. Mr. Chamberlain in fact spat upon me before the eyes of the world..."

"...It was in keeping with our own harmlessness that England took the liberty of some day meeting our peaceful activity with the brutality of the violent egoist."

"...The outstanding features of Polish character were cruelty and lack of moral restraint."

From a psychological point of view it is not too far-fetched to suppose that as the perversion developed and became more disgusting to Hitler's ego, its demands were disowned and projected upon the Jew. By this process the Jew became a symbol of everything which Hitler hated in himself. Again, his own personal problems and conflicts were transferred from within himself to the external world where they assumed the proportions of racial and national conflicts.

Forgetting entirely that for years he not only looked like a lower class Jew but was as dirty as the dirtiest and as great a social outcast, he now began to see the Jew as a source of all evil. The teachings of Schoenerer and Lueger helped to solidify and rationalize his feelings and inner convictions. More and more he became convinced that the Jew was a great parasite on humanity which sucked its life-blood and if a nation was to become great it must rid itself of this pestilence. Translated back into personal terms this would read: "My perversion is a parasite which sucks my life-blood and if I am to become great I must rid myself of this pestilence." When we see the connection between his sexual perversion and anti-Semitism, we can understand another aspect of his constant linking of syphilis with the Jew. These are the things which destroy nations and civilizations as a perversion destroys an individual.

Hitler
Psychological Analysis & Reconstruction

Part IV

The greater the demands of his perversion became, the more he hated the Jews and the more he talked against them. Everything which was bad was attributed to them. Here was his political career in an embryo state. He now spent most of his time reading books, attending political talks and reading newspapers in cafe houses. He himself tells us in so many words that he skipped through this material and only took out those parts which were useful to him. In other words, he was not reading and listening in order to become educated sufficiently to form a rational judgment of the problem. This would have been a violation of his earlier inhibition on thinking. He read only in order to find additional justification for his own inner feelings and convictions and to rationalize his projections. He has continued this technique up to the present time. He does a great deal of reading on many diverse subjects but he never forms a rational opinion in the light of the information but only pays attention to those parts which convince him that he was right to begin with.

In the evening he would return to his flophouse and harangue his associates with political and anti-Semitic speeches until he became a joke. This, however, did not disturb him too much. On the contrary, it seemed to act as a stimulant for further reading and the gathering of more arguments to prove his point of view. It was as though in trying to convince others of the dangers of Jewish domination, he was really trying to convince himself of the dangers of being dominated by his perversion. Perhaps Hitler is really referring to his perversion when he writes:

"During the long pro-war years of peace certain pathological features had certainly appeared. . .There were many signs of decay which ought to have stimulated serious reflection." (MK, 315)

The same may also be true when he says:

"How could the German people's political instincts become so morbid? The question involved here was not that of a single symptom, but instances of decay which flared up now in legion...which like poisonous ulcers ate into the nation now here, now there. It seemed as though a continuous flow of poison was driven into the farthest blood vessels of this one-time heroic body by a mysterious power, so as to lead to ever more severe paralysis of sound reason and of the simple instinct of self-preservation." (MK, 201)

As time went on the sexual stimulation of the Viennese environment seemed to aggravate the demands of his perversion. He suddenly became overwhelmed by the role that sex plays in the life of the lower classes and the Jews. Vienna became for him "the symbol of incest" and he suddenly left it to seek refuge with his ideal mother, Germany. But his pre-war days in Munich were not different from those he left behind in Vienna. His life was still one of extreme passivity and although we know little about them we can surmise that his days were filled with inner troubles.

The first World War.

Under these circumstances, we can understand why he thanked God for the first World War. For him it represented an opportunity of giving up his individual war against himself in exchange for a national war in which he would have the help of others. It also represented to him, on an unconscious level, an opportunity of redeeming his mother and assuming a masculine role for himself. Even at that time we may suppose he had inklings that he would be the Great Redeemer. It was not only his mother he was going to redeem, but also himself.

His advent in the German Army was really his first step in attempting to redeem himself as a social human being. No longer was he to be the underdog for he was joining forces with those who were determined to conquer and become great. Activity, replaced his earlier passivity to a large degree. Dirt, filth, and poverty were left behind and he could mingle with the chosen people on an equal footing. But for him this was not enough. As we. have pointed out in an earlier section, he was not content to be as clean as the average soldier. He had to go to the other extreme and become exceedingly clean. Whenever he returned from the front he immediately sat down and scrupulously removed every speck of mud from his person, much to the amusement of his comrades. Mend, his comrade during this time relates an experience at the front when Hitler upbraided one of the other men for not keeping himself clean and called him a "manure pile", which sounds very much like a memory of himself in Vienna.

During this period, as previously mentioned, his passive feminine tendencies were finding an outlet in his abasive conduct towards his officers. It looks as though he had not progressed sufficiently far in his conquest of himself to maintain a wholly masculine role. But with the help of others and the guidance of his respected officers he was making some progress toward what appeared to be a social adjustment. The final defeat of Germany, however, upset his well-laid plans and shattered his hopes and ambitions.

The defeat of Germany.

Nevertheless, it was this event which proved to be the turning-point in his life and determined that he would be an outstanding success rather than a total failure. UNconscious forces, some of which had been dormant for years, were now reawakened and upset his whole psychological equilibrium. His reaction to this event was an hysterical attack which manifested itself in blindness and mutism. Although the hysterical blindness saved him from witnessing what he regarded as an intolerable spectacle, it did not save him from the violent emotional reactions it aroused. These emotions, we may assume, were similar to those which he had experienced as a child when he discovered his aprents in intercourse. It seems logical to suppose that at that time he felt his mother was being defiled before his eyes but in view of his father's power and brutality he felt himself utterly helpless to redeem her honor or to save her from future assaults. If this is true, we would expect that he swore secret vengance against his father and, as has been shown, there is evidence to this effect.

Now the same thing was happening again but instead of his real mother it was his ideal mother, Germany, who was being betrayed, corrupted and humiliated and again he was unable to come to her rescue. A deep depression set in of which he writes:

> "What now followed were terrible days and even worse nights. Now I knew that everything was lost....In those nights my hatred arose, the hatred against the originators of this deed."

But again he was weak and helpless - a blind cripple lying in hospital. He struggled with the problem:

"How shall our nation be freed from the chains of this poisonous embrace?"

It would seem that the more he thought about it, the more his [unreadable] him that all was lost. He probably despised and condemned himself for his weakness and as his hatred continued to rise in the face of this frustrating experience he vowed ten and there:

"To know neither rest nor peace until the November Criminals had been overthrown..."

Undoubtedly his emotions were, extremely violent and would serve as a powerful motive for much of the retaliation which becomes so prominent in his later behavior. There are, however, many ways of retaliating which do not involve a complete upheaval and transformation of character such as we find in Hitler at this time.

From our experience with patients we know that complete transformations of this kind usually take place only under circumstances of extreme duress which demonstrate to the individual that his present character structure is no longer tenable. Naturally we do not know exactly what went on in Hitler's mind during this period or how he regarded his own position. We do how, however, that under such circumstances very strange thoughts and fantasies pass through the minds of relatively normal people and that in the case of neurotics, particularly when they have strong masochistic tendencies, these fantasies can become extremely absurd. Whatever the nature of these fantasies might have been, we may be reasonably sure that they involved his own safety or well-being. Only a danger of this magnitude would ordinarily cause an individual to abandon or revolutionize his character structure.

It may be that his nightmares will yield a clue. These, it may be remembered, center on the theme of his being attacked or subjected to indignities by another man. It is not his mother who is being attacked, but himself.

When he wakes from these nightmares he acts as though he were choking. He gasps for breath and breaks out in a cold sweat. It is only with great difficulty that he can be quieted again because frequently there is a hallucinatory after-effect and he believes he sees the man in his bedroom.

Under ordinary circumstances, we would be inclined to interpret this as the result of an unconscious wish for homosexual relations together with an ego revulsion against the latent tendency. This interpretation might apply to Hitler, too, for to some extent it seems as though he reacted to the defeat of Germany as a rape of himself as weel as of his symbolic mother. Furthermore, while he was lying helpless in the hospital, unable to see or to speak, he could well have considered himself an easy object for homosexual attack. When we remember, however, that for years he chose to live in a Vienna flophouse which was known to be inhabited by many homosexuals and later on associated with several notorious homosexuals, sych as Hess and Roehm, we cannot feel that this form of attack, alone, would be sufficient to threaten his integrity to such an extent that he would repudiate his former self.

A further clue to his thoughts during this period may be found in his great preoccupation with propaganda which, in his imagery is almost synonomous with poison.

"Slogan after slogan rained down on our people."

"...the front was flooded with this poison."

"...for the effect of its language on me was like that of spiritual vitrtol... I sometimes had to fight down the rage rising in me because of this concentrated solution of lies."

This type of imagery probably has a double significance. There is considerable evidence to show that as a child he believed that the man, during intercourse, injected poison into the woman which gradually destroyed her from within and finally brought about her death. Ths is not an uncommon belief in childhood and in view of the fact that his mother died from a cancer of the breast, after a long illness, the belief may have been more vivid and persisted longer in Hitler than in most children. On the other hand, the importance of poison in connection with his perversion has already been considered. We know about his inhibitions against taking certain substances into his mouth. These were not present during the early days of his career but developed much later in connection with his transformed character.

In view of all this it may not be too far-fetched to suppose that while he was fantasying *[error in original document]* about what the victors might do to the vanquished when they arrived, his masochistic and perverse tendencies conjured up the thought that they might attack him and force him to eat dung and drink urine (a practice which, it is alleged, is fairly common in Nazi concentration camps). Interestingly enough, this idea is incorporated in the colloquial expression "to eat the dirt of the victors." And in his weakened and helpless condition he would be unable to ward off such an attack. Such an hypothesis gains credence when we review the behavior of Nazi troops in the role of conquerors.

Transformation of character.

Although a thought of this kind would have certain pleasurable aspects to a masochistic person, it would also arouse fear of consequences together with violent feelings of guilt and disgust. If the thought kept recurring at frequent intervals and refused to be suppressed, we can easily imagine that it might drive an individual into such depths of despair that death would appear as the only solution. Hitler's fear of death has already been reviewed and it is possible that it was this alternative which shocked him out of his former self. Certain it is that in his public utterances, as well as in his actions, he attributes extraordinary powers to the fear of death.

> "I shall spread terror by the surprise employment of my measures. The important thing is the sudden shock of an overwhelming fear of death."

And in MEIN KAMPF he tells us that:

> "In the end, only the urge for self-preservation will eternally succeed. Under its pressure so-called 'humanity', as the expression of a mixture of stupidity, cowardice, and imaginary superior intelligence, will melt like snow under the March sun."

Sentiments of this sort suggest rather strongly that he was brought face to face with the prospect of his own death and that in order to save himself he had to rid himself of a bad conscience as well as the dictates of the intellect. The following quotations illustrate his attitude towards conscience and the need of rendering it inactive:

> "Only when the time comes when the race is no longer overshadowed by the consciousness of its own guilt, then it will find internal peace and external energy to cut down regardlessly and brutally the wild shoots, and to pull up the weeds."

> "Conscience is a Jewish invention. It is a blemish like circumcision."

> "I am freeing men from the restraints of an intelligence that has taken charge; from the dirty and degrading modifications of a chimera called conscience and morality"

And of the intellect he says:

"The intellect has grown autocratic and has become a disease of life,"

"We must distrust the intelligence and the conscience and must place our faith in our instincts."

Having repudiated these two important human functions, he was left almost entirely at the mercy of his passions, instincts and unconscious desires. At the crucial moment these forces durged to the fore in the form of an hallucination in which an inner voice informed him that he was destined to redeem the German people and lead them to greatness. This, for him, was a new view of life. It opened new vistas to him particularly in connection with himself. Not only did it confirm the vague feeling he had had since childhood, namely, that he was the "Chosen One" and under the protection of Providence, but also that he had been saved for a divine mission. This revelation served to crystallize his personality on a new pattern. He writes:

"In the hours of distress, when others despair, out of apparently harmless children, there shoots suddenly heros of death-defying determination and icy coolness of reflection. If this hour of trial had never come, then hardly anyone would ever have been able to guess that a young hero is hidden in the beardless boy. Nearly always such an impetus is needed in order to call genius into action. Fate's hammer-stroke, which then throws the one to the ground, suddenly strikes steel in another, and while now the shell of everyday life is broken, the erstwhile nucleus lies open to the eyes of the astonished world."

In another place he writes:

"A fire had been lighted, and out of its flames there was bound to come some day the sword which was to regain the freedom of the Germanic

Siegfried and the life of the German nation."

How, one may ask, was it possible for a person with Hitler's past life and abnormal tendencies to take this seriously? The answer is relatively simple. He believed it because he wanted to believe it - in fact, had to believe it in order to save himself. All the unpleasantries of the past he now interpreted as part of a great design. Just as it was Fate which ordained he should be born on the Austrian side of the border, so it was Fate which sent him to Vienna to suffer hardships in order to take the "milk-sop out of him by giving him Dame Sorrow as a foster-mother" and "kept him at the front where any negro could shoot him down when he could have rendered a much more worthwhile service elsewhere," and so it was probably Fate which decreed his past life and tendencies. These were the crosses he had to bear in order to prove his mettle. He might have been speaking about himself when he said of Germany:

> "...if this battle should not come, never would Germany win peace. Germany would decay and at the best would sink to ruin like a rotting corpse. But that is not our destiny. We do not believe that this misfortune which today our God sends over Germany has no meaning: it is surely the scourge which should and shall drive us to new greatness, to a new power and glory..."

Before. this new greatness, power ana glory could be achieved, however, it was necessary to conquer the misfortune. The misfortune in Hitler's case, so he probably thought, was the emotional identification he had made with his mother during childhood. He. had used this as a cornerstone for his personality which, instead of leading to greatness as he had hoped, had carried him to the brink of degradation, humiliation and self-destruction. It exposed him to untold dangers which were no longer compatible with self-preservation. Consequently, if we were to survive he must rid himself not only of his conscience and intellect but of all the traits which were associated with false "humanity". In its place he must set a personality which was in keeping with the "Law of Nature". Only after he had achieved this transformation could he feel safe from attack. To overcome his weakness and to grow strong became the dominant motive of his life.

> "...feels the obligation in accordance with the Eternal Will that dominates this universe to promote the Victory of the better and stronger, and to demand the Submission of the worse and weaker."

> "A stronger generation will drive out the weaklings because in its ultimate form the urge to live will again and again. break the ridiculous fetters of a socalled 'humanity' of the individual, so that its place will be taken by the 'humanity of nature', which destroys weakness in order to give its place to strength."

If our hypothesis concerning his mental processes while he lay helpless in Pasewalk Hospital is correct, we my assume that in order to quiet his fears he sometimes imagined himself as a person who far surpassed his enemies in all the "virile" qualities. Under these circumstances he could conquer his enemies and do to them what he now feared they would do to him. This is, of course, pure wishful thinking, but evidently this play of imagery yielded him so much pleasure that he unconsciously identified himself with this super-man image. We would guess that it was at the moment when this mechanism, which is known as "Identification with the Aggressor", operated, that the aforementioned hallucination was produced. He was no longer the weak and puny individual who was exposed to all kinds of attacks and indignities. On the contrary, he was fundamentally more powerful than all the others. Instead of his being afraid of them, they should be afraid of him.

The image Hitler created was a form of compensation for his own inferiorities, insecurities and guilts. Consequently the image negated all his former qualities and turned them into their opposites and to the same degree. All the human qualities of love, pity, sympathy and compassion were interpreted as weaknesses and disappeared in the transformation.

> "All passivity, all inertia (became) senseless, inimical to life."

> "The Jewish Christ-creed with its effeminate pity-ethics. '

> "Unless you are prepared to be pitiless you will get nowhere."

In their place we find what Hitler's warped mind conceived to be the super-masculine view:

> "...if a people is to become free it needs pride and will-power, defiance, hate, hate and once again hate."

> "Brutality is respected. Brutality and physical strength. The plain man in the street respects nothing but brutal strength and ruthlessness."

> "We want to be the supporters of the dictatorship of national reason, of national energy, of national brutality and resolution."

Anti-Semitism.

When the "Identification with the Aggressor" mechanism is used, however, there is no conscious struggle within the personality in which the new personality gradually overcomes the old one. The identification takes place outside the realm of consciousness and the individual suddenly feels that he is this new person. There is no process of integration or assimilation.

The old personality is automatically suppressed and its characteristics are projected onto some external object against which the new personality can carry on the struggle. In Hitler's case, all his undesirable characteristics were projected onto the Jew. To Hitler he became Evil incarnate and responsible for all the world's difficulties, just as Hitler's earlier femininity now appeared to him to be the source of all his personal difficulties, This projection was relatively easy for him to make inasmuch as in his Vienna days the Jew had become for him the symbol of sex, disease and his perversion. Now another load of undesirable qualities was poured upon his head with the result that Hitler now hated and despised the Jew with the same intensity as he hated his former self.

Obviously, Hitler could not rationalize his projection as long as he stood by himself as a single individual, nor could he combat the Jew single-handed. For this he needed a large group which would fit the picture he had created. He found this in defeated Germany as a whole. At the close of the war it was in a position almost identical with his own before the transformation had taken place. It, too, was weak and exposed to further attack and humiliation. It, too, had to be prepared to eat the dirt of the conquerors and during the inflation period, it, too, was confused, pasive and helpless. It, therefore, made an excellent symbol of his earlier self and Hitler again shifted his personal problems to a national and racial scale where he could deal with them more objectively. Providence had "given" him the spark which transformed him over-night. It was now his mission to transform the remainder of the German people by winning them to his view of life and the New Order. The Jews now played the same role in the life of Germany as his effeminate, masochistic and perverse adjustment had played in his own life. He now resolved to become a politician.

Many writers have expressed the opinion that Hitler's anti-Semitism is motivated primarily by its great propaganda value. Undoubtedly, anti-Semitism is the most powerful weapon in his propaganda arsenal and Hitler is well aware of it. He has even expressed the opinion on several occasions that the Jews would make Germany rich. All our informants who knew him well, however, agree that this is superficial and that underneath he has a sincere hatred for the Jews and everything Jewish. This is in complete agreement with our hypothesis. We do not deny that he often uses anti-Semitism porpagandistically when it suits his purpose. We do maintain, however, that behind this superficial motivation is a much deeper one which is largely unconscious. Just as Hitler had to exterminate his former self in order to get the feeling of being great and strong, so must Germany exterminate the Jews if it is to attain its new glory. Both are poisons which slowly destroy the respective bodies and bring about death.

> "All great cultures of the past perished only because the originally creative race died off through blood-poisoning."

> "...alone the loss of purity of the blood destroys the inner happiness forever; it eternally lowers man, and never again can its consequences be removed from body and mind."

The symbolism in tehse quotations is obvious and the frequency with which they recur in his speaking and writing bears testimony to their great importance in his thinking and feeling processes. It would seem from this that unconsciously he felt that if he succeeds in ridding himself of his personal poison, his effeminate and perverse tendencies as symbolized in the Jew, then he would achieve immortality.

In his treatment of the Jews we see the "Identification with the Aggressor" mechanism at work. He is now practicing on the Jews in reality the things he feared the victors might do to him in fantasy. From this he derives a manifold satisfaction. First, it affords him an opportunity of appearing before the world as the pitiless brute he imagines himself to be; second, it affords him an opportunity of proving to himself that he is as heartless and brutal as he wants to be (that he can really take it); third, in eliminating the Jews he unconsciously feels that he is ridding himself, and Germany, of the poison which is responsible for all difficulties; fourth, as the masochist he really is, he derives a vicarious pleasure from the suffering of others in whom he can see himself; fifth, he can give vent to his bitter hatred and contempt of the world in general by using the Jew as a scapegoat; and sixth, it pays heavy material and propagandistic dividends.

Early political career.

Armed with this new view of life Hitler sought for opportunities to put his resolve to become a politician into effect and start on the long road which would redeem Germany and lead her to new greatness and glory. This was not easy in post-war Germany which was now engaged in violent internal strife He remained in the Reserve Army for a time where he engaged in his "first political activity" – that of spying on his comrades. His duties were to mingle with the men in his barracks and engage them in political discussions. Those who voiced opinions with a Communict flavor he reported to his superior officers. Later, when the offenders were brought to trial, it was his job to take the witness stand and give the testimony which would sent these comrades to their death. This was a severe trial for his new character but he carried it off in a brazen and unflinching manner. It must have given him tremendous satisfaction to find that he actually could play this new role in such an admirable fashion. Not long afterwards it was discovered that he had a talent for oratory and he was rewarded for his service by being promoted to instructor. The new Hitler, the embryo Fuehrer, was beginning to pay dividends.

"Identification with the Agressor" is, at best, an

unstable form of adjustment. The individual always has a vague feeling that something is not as it should be, although he is not aware of its origins. Nevertheless, he feels insecure in his new role and in order to rid himself of his uneasiness he most prove to himself, over and over again, that he is really the type of person he believes himself to be. The result is a snow-ball effect. Every brutality must be followed by a greater brutality, every violence by a greater violence, every atrocity by a great atrocity, every gain in power by a greater gain in power, and so on down the line. Unless this is achieved successfully, the individual begins to feel insecure and doubts concerning his borrowed character begin to creep in together with feelings of guilt regarding his shortcomings. This is the key to an understanding of Hitler's actions since the beginning of his political activities to the present day. This effect has not escaped the attention of non-psychological observers. Francois-Poncet, for example, writes in the French Yellow Book:

> "The Chancellor chafes against all these disappointments with indignant impatience. Far from conducing him to moderation, these obstacles irritate him. He is aware of the enormous blunder which the anti-Jewish persecutions of last November have proved to be; yet, by a contradiction which is part of the dictator's psychological make-up, he is said to be preparing to enter upon a merciless struggle against the Church and Catholicism. Perhaps he thus wishes to wipe out the memory of past violence with fresh violence..." (p. 49)

The mechanism feeds on itself and must continue to grow in order to maintain itself. Since it has no real foundations to support it, the individual can never quite convince himself that he is secure and need fear no longer. The result is that he can brook no delays but must plunge ahead on his mad career.

Hitler's political career shows these tendencies to a marked degree. Scarcely had he affiliated himself with the group which had founded the Party than he connived to get control over it. Then followed a rapid expansion of membership, the introductiom of terror, a series of broken promises, collusions and betrayals. Each brought him fresh gains and new power, but the pace was still too slow to satisfy him. In 1923 he believed himself to be strong enough to undertake a Putsch and seize the reins of government. The Putsch failed and Hitler's conduct during it has been the subject of much comment. There are a number of versions c oncerning what happened. Some report that when the troops fired on them Hitler fell to the ground and crawled through an alley which carried him to safety while Ludendorff, Roehm and Goering marched ahead. Some claim that he stumbled, others that he was knocked down by his bodyguard who was killed. The Nazi version is that he stopped to pick up a small child who had run out into the street and been knocked down! Years later they produced a child on the anniversary of the event to prove the story!

From a psychological point of view it would appear that he turned coward on this occasion and that he did fall down and crawl away from the scene of activities. Although he had usurped considerable power and had reason to have faith in his new character, it seems unlikely that it was sufficient for him to actually engage the recognized authority in physical combat. His attitude towards recognized superiors and authority in general would make such a direct attack improbable. Furthermore, his reactions after his escape would seem to indicate that his new role had temporarily failed. He went into a deep depression and was restrained from committing suicide only by constant reassurances. When he was taken to Landsberg prison he went on a hunger strike and refused to eat for three weeks. This was his response to being placed again in the position of the vanquished. Perhaps memories of his fantasies in the hospital were returning to harass him! It was only after he discovered that his jailers were not unkindly disposed to him that, he permitted himself to be persuaded to take food.

During his stay in Landsberg he became much quieter. Ludecke says:

> "Landsberg had done him a world of good. Gone from his manner was the nervous intensity which formerly had been his most unpleasant characteristic."

It was during this period, that he wrote MEIN KAMPF and we may suppose that his failure in the Putsch made it necessary for him to take a fresh inventory and integrate his new character more firmly. He resolved, at this time, not to try another Putsch in the future but to gain the power by legal means alone! In other words, he would not participate again in an open conflict with the recognized authority.

His rise to power.

It is scarcely necessary for us to trace the history of his rise to power and his actions after he achieved it. They all follow along the same general pattern we have outlined. Each successful step served to convince him that he was the person he believed himself to be but brought no real sense of security. In order to attain this he had to go a step higher and give additional proof that he was not deluding himself. Terror, violence and ruthlessness grew with each advance and every recognized virtue was turned into a vice - a sign of weakness. Even after he became the undisputed leader of the nation, he could not rest in peace. He projected his own insecurities onto the neighboring states and then demanded that they bow to his power. As long as there was a nation or a combination of nations more powerful than Germany, he could never find the peace and security h' longed for. It was inevitable that this course would lead to war because only by that means could he crush the threat and prove to himself that he need no longer be afraid. It was also inevitable that the war would be as brutal and pitiless as possible for only in this way could he prove to himself that he was not weakening in his chosen course but was made of stuff becoming to his conception of what a victor should be.

Rages.

Although space will not permit a detailed analysis of the operation of the various psychological streams we have enumerated, in the determination of his everyday behavior, a few have aroused sufficient speculation to warrant a place in our study. One of the outstanding of these is his rages. Most writers have regarded these as temper-tantrums, his reaction to minor frustrations and deprivations. On the surface they appear to be of this nature and yet, when we study his behavior carefully, we find that when he is confronted by a real frustration or deprivation, such as failure to be elected to the Presidency or being refused the Chancellorship, his behvaior is exactly the opposite. He is very cool and quiet. He is disappointed but not enraged. Instead of carrying on like a spoiled child, he begins immediately to lay plans for a new assault. Heiden, his biographer, describes his characteristic pattern as follows:

> "When others after a defeat would have gone home despondently, consoling themselves with the philosophic reflection that it was no use contending against adverse circumstances, Hitler delivered a second and a third assault with sullen defiance. When others after a success would have become more cautious, because they would not dare put fortune to the proof too often and perhaps exhaust it, Hitler persisted and staked a bigger claim on Destiny with every throw."

This does not sound like a person who would fly into a rage at a trifle.

Nevertheless, we know that he does fly into these rages

and launches into tirades on very slight provocation. If we examine the causes of these outbursts, we almost invariably find that the trigger which sets them off is something which he considers to be a challenge of his super-man personality. It may be a contradiction, a criticism or even a doubt concerning the truth or wisdom of something he has said or done, or it might be a slight or the anticipation of opposition. Even though the subject may be trifling or the challenge only by implication, or even wholly imagined, he feels called upon to display his primitive character. Francois-Poncet has also detected and described this reaction. He writes:

"Those who surround him are the first to admit that he now think himself infallible and invincible. That explains why he can no longer bear either criticism or contradiction. To contradict him is in his eyes a crime of 'lese-majeste'; opposition to his plans, from whatever it may come, is a definite sacrilege, to which the only reply is an immediate and striking display of his omnipotence."

As soon as his display has served its purpose and cowed his listeners into submission, it is turned off as suddenly as it was turned on. How great is the insecurity which demands such constant vigilence and apprehension!

Fear of domination.

We find this same insecurity at work when he is meeting new people and particularly those to whom he secretly feels inferior in some way. Earlier in our study we had occasion to point out that his eyes had taken over a diffuse sexual function. When he first meets the person he fixates him with his eyes as though to bore through the other person. There is a peculiar glint in them on these occasions which may have been interpreted as an hypnotic quality. To be sure, he uses them in such a way and tries to over-power the other person with them. If he turns his eyes away, Hitler keeps them fixed directly on him or her but if the other person returns this gaze Hitler turns his away and looks up at the ceiling as long as the interview continues. It is as though he were mtching his power against theirs. If he success in overpowering the other person, he rudely follows up his advantage. If, however, the other person refuses to succumb to his glance, he avoids the possibility of succumbing to theirs. Likewise, he is unable to match wits with another person in a straightforward argument. He will express his opinion at length but will not defend it on logical grounds. Strasser says:

> "He is afraid of logic. Like a woman he evades the issue and ends by throwing in your face an argument entirely remote from what you were talking about."

We might suspect that even on this territory he cannot expose himself to a possible defeat which would mar the image he has of himself. He is, in fact, unable to face real opposition on any ground. He cannot speak to a group in which he senses opposition but walks out on his audience. He has run out of meetings with Ludendorff, Gregor Strasser, Bavarian Industrialists, and many others, because he could not risk the possibility of appearing in an inferior light or expose himself to a possible domination by another person. There is reason to suppose that his procrastination is not so much a matter of laziness as it is a fear of coming to grips with a difficult problem. Consequently, he avoids it as long as possible and it is only whe! the situation has become dangerous and disaster lies ahead that his "inner voice" or intuition communicates with him and tells him what course he should follow. Most of his thinking is carried on subconsciously which probably accounts for his ability to penetrate difficult problems and time his moves. Psychological experiments in this field seem to indicate that on this level the individual is often able to solve very complex problems which are impossible him on the level of consciousness. Whenever

we turn in studying Hitler's behavior patterns we find the spectre of possible defeat and humiliation as one of his dominant motivations.

Monuments.

His passion for constructing huge buildings, stadia, bridges, roads, etc., can only be interpreted as attempts to compensate fbr his lack of confidence. These are tangible proofs of his greatness which are designed to impress himself as well as others. Just as he must be the greatest man in all the world, so he has a tendency to build the greatest and biggest of everything. Most of the structures he has erected he regards as temporary buildings. They are, to his way of thinking, on a par with ordinary mortals. The permanent buildings he plans to construct later on. They will be much larger and grander and will be designed to last at least a thousand years. In other words, these are befitting monuments to himself who plans on ruling the German people for that period of time through his new view of life.

It is also interesting to note the frequency with which he uses gigantic pillars in all his buildings. Most of the buildings are almost surrounded by them and he places them in every conceivable place. Since pillars of this sort are almost universally considered to be phallic symbols, we may regard the size and frequency as unconscious attempts to compensate for his own impotence. His huge pageants serve a similar purpose.

Oratory.

No study oh Hitler would be complete without mentioning his oratory talents. His extraordinary gift for swaying large audiences has contributed, perhaps more than any other single factor, to his success and the rartial realization of his ideal. In order to understand the power of his appeal, we must be cognizant of the fact that for him the masses are fundamentally feminine in character. To Hanfstaengl and other informations he has

frequently said, "Die Masse ist ein Weib", and in MEIN KAMPF he writes:

> "The people, in an overwhelming majority, are so feminine in their nature and attitude that their activities and thoughts are motivated less by sober consideration than by feeling and sentiment."

In other words, his uconscious frame of reference, when addressing a huge audience, is fundamentally that of talking to a woman.

In spite of this, his insecurities assert themselves. He never is the first speaker on the program. He must always have a speaker precede him who warms up the audience for him. Even then he is nervous and jittery when he gets up to speak. Frequently he has difficulty in finding words with which to begin. He is trying to get the "feel" of the audience. If it "feels"' favorable, he starts in a rather cautious manner. His tone of voice is quite normal and he heals [error in original document] with his material in a fairly objective manner. But as he proceeds his voice begins to rise and his tempo increases. If the response of the audience is good, his voice becomes louder and louder and the tempo faster and faster. By this time all objectivity has disappeared and passion has taken complete possession of him. The mouth which can never utter a fragment of profanity off the speaker's platform now pours forth a veritable stream of curses, foul names, vilification and hatred. Hafstaengl compaes the development of a Hitlerian speech with the development of a Wagnerian theme which may account for Hitler's love of Wagnerian music and the inspiration he derives from it.

This steady stream of filth continues to pour forth until both he and the audisnce are in a frenzy. When he stops he is on the verge of exhaustion. His breathing is heavy and uncontrolled and he is wringing wet with perspiration. Many writers have commented on the sexual

components in his speaking and some have described the climax as a veritable orgasm. Heyst writes:

> "In his speeches we hear the suppressed voice of passion and wooing which is taken from the language of love; he utters a cry of hate and voluptousness, a spasm of violence and cruelty. All those tones and sounds are taken from the back-streets of the instincts; they remind us of dark impulses repressed too long."

And Hitler himself says:

> "Passion alone will give to him, who is chosen by her, the words that, like beats of a hammer, are able to open the doors to the heart of a people."

Undoubtedly, he uses speaking as a means of talking himself into the super-man role and of living out the role of "Identification with the Agressor". He carefully builds up imposing enemies - Jews, Bolsheviks, capitalists, democracies, etc., in order to demolish them without mercy (these are all inventions of the Jews to his way of thinking and consequently in attacking any one of them he is fundamentally attacking the Jews). Under these circumstances. He appears to the naive and unsophisticated listener as the Great Redeemer of Germany.

But that is only one side of the picture. On the other side we have the sexual attack which, in his case, is of a perverse nature. It finds expression in his speaking but due to the transformation of character everything appears in reverse. The steady stream of filth he pours on the heads of his "feminine" audience is the reverse of his masochistic perversion which finds gratification in having women pour their "filth" on him. Even the functions of the physical organs is reversed. The mouth which, under ordinary circumstances, is an organ of injection and is surrounded with inhibitions and prohibitions, now becomes the organ through which filth is ejected. Hitler's speaking has been aptly described as a "verbal diarrhea". Rauschning describes it as an oral enema. It is probably this unconscious sexual element in his speaking which holds such a fascination for many people.

His appeal.

A word may be added in connection with the content of his speeches. Strasser sums it up very concisely when he says:

> "Hitler responds to the vibrations of the human heart with the delicacy of a seismograph... enabling him, with a certainty with which no conscious gift could endow him, to act as a loudspeaker proclaiming the most secret desires, the least permissible instincts, the sufferings and personal revolts of a whole nation."

We are now in a position to understand how this is possible for him. In regarding his audience as fundamentally feminine in character, his appeal is directed at a repressed part of their personalities. In many of the German people there seems to be a strong feminine-masochistic tendency which is usually covered over by more "virile'" characteristics but which finds partial gratification in submissive behavior, discipline, sacrifice, etc. Nevertheless, it does seem to disturb them and they try to compensate for it by going to the other extreme of courage, pugnaciousness, determination, etc. Most Germans are unaware of this hidden part of their personalities and would deny its existence vehemently if such an insinuation is made. Hitler, however, appeals to it directly and he is in an excellent position to know what goes on in that region because in him this side of personality was not only conscious but dominant throughout his earlier life.

Furthermore, these tendencies were far more intense in him than in the average person and he had a better opportunity of observing their operation. In addressing an audience in this way he need only dwell on the longings, ambitions, hopes and desires of his earlier life in order to awaken these hidden tendencies in his listeners. This he does with inordinate skill. In this way he is able to arouse the same attitudes and emotions in his listeners that he himself now experiences in connection with this type of adjustment, and is able to direct these into the same channels that he has found useful. Thus he is able to win them to his new view of life which sets a premium on brutality, ruthlessness, dominance, determination, etc., and which frowns upon all the established human qualities. The key throughout will be to strive to be what you are not and to do your best to exterminate that which you are. The behavior of the German armies has been an outstanding manifestation of this contradiction. To the psychologist it seems as though the brutality expressed towards the people of the , occupied countries is motivated not only by a desire to prove to themselves that they are what they are not, but also by, a vicarious masochistic gratification which they derive from an identification with their victims. On the whole, one could say of many of the German troops what Rauschning said of Hitler:

"...there lies behind Hitler's emphasis on brutality and ruthlessness the desolation of a forced and artificial inhumanity, not the amorality of the genuine brute, which has after all something of the power of a natural force."

Hitler's Probable Behavior in the Future

As the tide of battle turns against Hitler it may be well to consider very briefly the possibilities of his future behavior and the effect that each would have on the German people as well as on ourselves.

1. Hitler may die of natural causes.

This is only a remote possibility since, as far as we

know, he is in fairly good health except for his stomach ailment which is, in all probability, a psychosomatic disturbance. The effect such an event would have on the German people would depend on the nature of the illness which brought about his death. If he would die from whooping cough, mumps, or some other ridiculous disease, it would be a material help in breaking the myth of his supernatural origins.

2. Hitler might seek refuge in a neutral country.

This is extremely unlikely in view of his great concern about his immortality. Nothing would break the myth more effectively than to have the leader run away at the critical moment. Hitler knows this and has frequently condemned the Kaiser for his flight to Holland at the close of the last war. Hitler might want to escape as he has escaped from other unpleasant situations, but it seems almost certain that he would restrain himself.

3. Hitler might get killed in battle.

This is a real possibility. When he is convinced that he cannot win, he may lead his troops into battle and expose himself as the fearless and fanatical leader. This would be most undesirable from our point of view because his death would serve as an example to his followers to fight on with fanatical, death-defying determination to the bitter end. This would be what Hitler would want for he has predicted that:

> "We shall not capitulate...no, never. We my be destroyed, but if we are, we shall drag a world with us...a world in flames." .

> "But even if we could not conquer them, we should drag half the world into destruction with us and leave no one to triumph over Germany. There will not be another 1918."

At a certain point he could do more towards the achievement

of this goal by dying heroically than he could by living. Furthermore, death of this kind would do more to bind the German people to the Hitler legend and insure his immortality than any other course he could pursue.

4. Hitler might be assassinated.

Although Hitler is extremely well protected there is a possibility that someone may assassinate him. Hitler is afraid of this possibility and has expressed the opinion that:

> "His own friends would one day stab him mortally in the back... And it would be just before the last and greatest victory, at the moment of supreme tension. Once more Hagen would slay Siegfried. Once more Hermann the Liberator would be murdered by his own kinsmen. The eternal destiny of the German nation must be fulfilled yet again, for the last time."

This possibility too, would be undesirable from our point of view inasmuch as it would make a martyr of him and strengthen the legend.

It would be even more undesirable if the assassin were a Jew for this would convince the German people of Hitler's infallibility and strengthen the fanaticism of the German troops and people. Needless to say, it would be followed by the complete extermination or all Jews in Germany and the occupied countries.

5. Hitler may go insane.

Hitler has many characteristics which border on the schizophrenic. It is possible that when faced with defeat his psychological structure may collapse and leave him at the mercy of his unconscious forces. The possibilities of such an outcome diminish as he becomes older, but they should not be entirely excluded. This would not be an undesirable eventuality from our point of view since it would do much to undermine he Hitler legend in the minds of the German people.

6. German military might revolt and seize him.

This seems unlikely in view of the unique position Hitler holds in the minds of the German people. From all the evidence it would seem that Hitler alone is able to rouse the troops, as well as the people to greater efforts and as the road becomes more difficult this should be an important factor. One could imagine, however, that as defeat approaches Hitler's behavior may become more and more neurotic and reach a point where it would be well for the military to confine him. In this case, however, the German people would probably never know about it.

If they discovered it, it would be a desirable end from our point of view because it would puncture the myth of the loved and invincible leader.

The only other possibility in this connection would be that the German military should decide, in the face of defeat, that it might be wiser to dethrone Hitler and set up a puppet government to sue for peace. This would probably cause great internal strife in Germany. What the ultimate outcome might be would depend largely on the manner in which it was handled and what was done with Hitler. At the present time the possibility seems extremely remote.

7. Hitler may fall into our hands.

This is the most unlikely possibility of all. Knowing his fear of being placed in the role of the vanquished, we can imagine that he would do his utmost to avoid such a fate. From our point of view it would not be undesirable.

8. Hitler might commit suicide.

This is the most plausible outcome. Not only has he frequently threatened to commit suicide, but from what we know of his psychology it is the most likely possibility. It is probably true that he has an inordinate fear of death, but being an hysteric he could undoubtedly screw himself up into the super-man character and perform the deed. In all porbability, however, it would not be a simple suicide. He has too much of the dramatic for that and since immortailty is one of his dominant motives we can imagine that he would stage the most dramatic and effective death scene he could possibly think of. He knows how to bind the people to him and if he cannot have the bond in life he will certainly do his utmost to achieve it in death. He might even engage some other fanatic to do the final killing at his orders.

Hitler has already envisaged a death of this kind, for he has said to Rauschning:

> "Yes, in the hour of supreme peril I must sacrifice myself for the people."

This would be extremely undesirable from our point of view because if it is cleverly done it would establish the Hitler legend so firmly in the minds of the German people that it might take generations to eradicate it.

Whatever else happens, we my be reasonably sure that as Germany suffers successive defeats Hitler will become more and more neurotic. Each defeat will shake his confidence still further and limit his opportunities for proving his own greatness to himself. In consequence he will feel himself more and more vulnerable to attack from his associates and his rages will increase in frequency. He will probably try to compensate for his vulnerability on this side by continually stressing his brutality and ruthlessness.

His public appearances will become less and less for, as we have seen, he is unable to face a critical audience. He will probably seek solace in his Eagle's Nest on the Kehlstein near Berchtsegaden. There among the ice-capped peaks he will wait for his "inner voice" to guide him. Meanwhile, his nightmares will probably increase in frequency and intensity and drive him closer to a nervous collapse. It is not wholly improbably that in the end he might lock himself into this symbolic womb and defy the world to get him.

In any case, his mental condition will continue to deteriorate. He will fight as long as he can with any weapon or technique that can be conjured up to meet the emergency. The course he will follow will almost certainly be the one which seems to him to be the surest road to immortality and at the same time drag the world down in flames.

COMPLETE BIBLIOGRAPHY

Names preceded by asterisk have been excerpted and are included in the Hitler Source-Book.

ABEL, Theodor: Why Hitler came into Power? New York, Prentice Hall Inc.1938.

ADAM, Adela M., Philip alias Hitler. Oxford, 1941, v. 10. p. 105-113

ALLARD, Paul: Quand Hitler espionne la France., Paris. Les editions de France. 1939. 197 p.

*ANDERNACH, Andreas: Hitler ohne Maske. Munchen. Der Antifaschist. 1932.

ARBUERSTER, Martin: Adolf Hitler, Blut oder Geist. Zurich. Reso Verlag. 1936. 47 p. Kulturpolit. Schriften Heft 7.

ATLANTIC MONTHLY - FAIRWEATHER, N.: Hitler and Hitlerism. 149: 380-87, 509-16, March-April 1932.

       "   FAIRWEATHER, N.: A man of destiny. 149 vol. 380-87.

BADE, Wilfid: Der Weg des Dritten Reichs. 4 Bande Lubeek, Coleman. 1933-38, je 150 Seiten.

BAINVILLE, Jacques: Histoire de deux peuples, continuue jusqu'a Hitler. Paris. Flammarion. 1938. 155 p.

*BALK, Ernst, Wilhelm: "Mein Fuhrer". Berlin. P. Schmidt. 1935. 15 p.

*BAVARIAN State Police: Report to the Bavarian State Ministry of the Interior Re: Conditional Parole of Adolf Hitler.

*BAYLES, Will D.: Caesars in Goose Step. New York, Harper Bros. 1940.
262 p.

*BAYNES, Helton Godwins: "Germany possessed", London. J. Cape. 1941.

*BEDEL, Maurice: Monsieru Hitler (17 ieme ed.) Paris. Gallinard. 1937.
92 p.

BELGIUM. The Official Account of What Happened. 1939-40. Belgium.
New York. 1941.

*BERCHTHOLD, Josef: Hitler Uber Deutschland. Munchen. F. Eher 1932
88 p.

BEREITSCHAFT fur Adolf Hitler. Wien 1932.15 p.

*BERLINER ILLUSTRIERTE ZEITUNG. Berline No. 32. August, 1939.
Militarpass Adolf Hitlers.

*BERLINER TAGEBLATT: Berlin 2/27/1924 p. 10-26. Putschprozess
                                        Hitlers Vernehmung

       "   "   : Berlin Sept. 6, 1930. Hitler als
                                          Zeuge im Leipziger
                                          Reischwahrprozess

*BERTRAND, Louis, M.E.: ... Hitler. Paris. Fayard & Cie. 1936

*BILLINGER, Karl (pseud.). Hitler is no fool". Modern age books. 1939

*BILLUNG, R.: Rund um Hitler. Munchen. 1931. B. Funck.

BLAKE, Leonard: Hitler's last year of Power. London A. Daker's Ltd.
1939.

*BLANK, Herbert: Adolf Hitler, Wilhelm III. Berlin Rowohlt. 1931. 92 p.

BOUHLER, Phillip: ...Adolf Hitler, Das WERDEN einer Volksbewegung.
                        (Colemans K.Biogr. Heft. 11. 1935. 49 p.)

   "   "   : Adolf Hitler, a short sketch of his life.
                                     Terramare office. 1938

BRADY, Robert A.: The Spirit and Structure of German Fascism. New York,
1937.

BRAUN, Otto: Von Weimar zu Hitler. New York, Europa Verl. 1940.

BREDOW, Klaus: Hitler rast. Der 20. Juni ... Saarbrucken ? 1934. 72 p.

BRENTANO, Bernard: Der Beginn der Barbarei in Deutschland. Rowohlt.
Berlin. 1930.

*BRITISH WAR BLUE BOOK. 1939

BROOKS, Robert CLarkson: ...Deliver us from Dictators. University of
Penna. Press. 1935, 245 p.

*BUELOW, Paul: Adolf Hitler und der Bayreuther Kulturkreis.
(Aus Deutschlands Werden. Heft 9. p, 1-16) Leipzig 1935.

CAHEN, Max: Men against Hitler. Dobbs & Merrill. May, 1939.

CANADIAN MONTHLY: LE COURDAIS, D.N.: Crackpot Chancellor. 91:20-22
April 1939.

CATHOLIC WORLD-[unreadable] P.: Masterstroke of Psychology.

148:190-97 November, 1938.

*   "   "   " :HUDDLESTON, S.: Hitler the Orator. 149
                                 229/30 May, 1939.

       "   "   GILLIS, J.M.: Austrian Phaeton.
                             151:257-65 Jan. 1940

CHATEAUBRIANT, Alphonse, de: ...La Gerbe des Forces. Noucelle Allemagne,
    1937.

*CHELIUS, Fritz, Heinz: Aus Hitlers Jugenland und Jugendzeit.
    Leipzig. Schaufuss. 1933. 30 p.

CHRISTIAN CENTURY-CLINCHY, E.R.: I saw Hitler, too. 49:1131-33
                                September 21, 1932

       "   "   :[unreadble] , E.G.: Hitler and German Religion.
                                 50:418-20 - March 29, 1933.

       "   "   : HUTCHINSON, P.: Portent of Hitler.
                                 50:1299-1301 October 18, 1933.

       "   "   :PENDELL, E.H.: Adolph alias 666.50:759.
                                 January 7, 1933. Discussion 50:818,849.
                                 January 21-28, 1933.

       "   "   : RAMSDELL, E.T.: Hitler adored and hated.
                                 51:971. July 25, 1934

CHRISTIAN CENTURY (cont.)   : How seriously must Hitler be taken.
                                 53.1277 September 30, 1936.

       "   "   : Comedy has its limits: Chaplinized Hitler
                                 57:816-17 January 26. 1940.

*CIALATINI, Franco: Hitler e il Fascismo.R.Bemporad, Firenze. 1933 70 p.

CLINCHY, Everett R.: The Strange Case of Herr Hitler.
    The John Day Pamphlets. No. 24, 1933. 30 p.

COLLIER's - YBARRA, T.R.: Says Hitler, Interview. 29:17, July 1, 1933

       "   "   : Hitler. 94-50. August 4, 1934.

       "   HANFSTAENGL, E.T.S.: My Leader. 94. 7-9 August 4, 1934.

       "   YBARRA, T.R.: Hitler changes his clothes. 95:12/3 April 27,
                                 1935.

       "   "   : Hitler on High. 100:21/2 September 4, 1937

       "   CHURCHILL, W. : Dictators are Dynamite. 102: 16/7
                                 September 3, 1938.

                      "   : Is Hitler Crazy? 103:82. June 17, 1939.

       "   BLOCH, E.   : My Patient Hitler. 107:11, March. 15, 1941,
                                 69-70, March 22, 1941.

       "   OECHSNER, F. : Portable Lair: Fuehrerhauptquartie. 110:26
                                 August 22, 1942.

COMMONWEAL: Quandaries of Herr Hitler. 16:419. August 31, 1.932.

       "   - BINSSE, H.L. : Complete Hitler. 29:625/6. March 31, 1939.

CONTEMPORARY REVIEW: Adolf Hitler. 140:726-32, December 1931.

EXCERPT.R.of Rs. 85:56/7. February 1932.
  "   "   : Hitler's Age of Heroism. The Advent of
             Herr Hitler. 143. vol. 532-41, 143
             vol. 366-68, 1933.

  "   "   : Hitler's Cards. Germanicus. 154:190-96,
             August 1938.

CONTEMPORARY REVIEW (cont.): Der Fuhrer Spricht. 155; 357-88, Marchh 1939

  "   "   STERN-RUBARTH, E.: Heinrich Himmler,
             Hitler's Fouche, Head of Gestapo.
             158: 641-48, December 1940.

  "   "   ALBERT, E.: Hitler and Mussolini. 159:155-61,
             February, 1941.

*CRAIN, Maurice: Rulers of the World. New York, 1940.

CURRENT HISTORY: - LORRE, L.: Hitler's Bid for German Power. May, 1932

  "   "   : FRITERS, G.: Who are the German
             Fascists? 35:532-36, January, 1932.

* "   "   : PHAYRE, I: Holiday with Hitler. 44:50-58,
             July 1936.

  "   "   : Prosecuted by Hitler, an unbiased Account
             of a real [unreadable]. 44:83-90, June 1936.

  "   "   : Mr. Hitler. 48:74/5. January, 1938.

  "   "   : Dictatorial Complex; Psychologist
             analyses the mental pattern of Europe's
             strongest strong Men. J. Jastrow. 49:40
             December 1, 1938.

  "   "   : PANTON, S.: Hitler's New Hiding Place. 50:71/2
             April. 1939.

  "   "   : Hitler's Escape. 51:12. December. 1939.

  "   "   : Hitler as Wotan...Retreat High Bavarian Alps.
             by T. Lang 51:50. February 1, 1940.

  "   "   : Stranger in Paris. 51:54 August, 1940.

  "   "   : Asaetic Adolf; Hitler' s Income. 52:27/28. January
             23, 1941.

* "   "   : I Was Hitler's Boss. Volume I- November 1941.
             p. 193/99.

*CZECH-JOCHBERG, Erich: Adolf Hitler und seinsteb. Oldenburg. G
 Stalling, 1933.

*   " : Hitler, eine Deutsche Bewegung. Oldenburg.
            Stalling, 1936.

D'ABERNON, Edgar, Vincent: Diary of an Ambassador. 1920/26,
 New York, Doubleday.

*DESCAVES, Pierre: Hitler. Paris. Dencel & Steele. 1936.

*DEUEL, Wallace R.: People under Hitler. New York. Harcourt...1942
 p. 92.

DEUTSCHE Juristenzeitung. 330. Oktober, 1924. Munchener Hochverratsprozess. Graf zu Dohna.

DEUTSCHE Republik. V.4. 1930. Riesse, G. Hitler und die Armee.

"   "   V.358-64. Das Schutzserum gegen die Hitlerei.

"   "   V. 1476-81 Figuren aus dem "Dritten Reich".

DIEBOW, Hans: Hitler, eine Biographie. W. Kolk. 1931

*DIETRICH, Otto: Mit Hitler in die Macht. F. Eher Nachfl. Munchen.
     1934. p. 209.

*DOBERT, Eitel Wolf: Convert to Freedom, New York, Putnam's, 1940.

*DODD'S, Ambassador: Diary. 1933-38. New York - Harcourt,1941. 464 p.

*DODD, Martha: Through Embassy Eyes. New York, Harcourt, 1939. 382 p.

[unreadable], Eugen: Mussolini, Hitler .. Leipzig. S. Schnurpfeil
     Verlag. 1931, 16 p.

DOKUMENTE DER DEUTSCHER POLITIK, Berlin, Junker & Dunnhaupt
     Verlag. 1935-39.

DUHAMEL, Georges: Memoriel de la Guerre Blanche. 1936, Paris. 1939

*DUTCH, Oswald (pseud.) Hitler's12 Apostles. London. E. Arnold & Co.
     1939, 271 p.

DZELEPY, E.N.: ... Hitler contra la France ? Paris. Editions Excelsior, 1933.
          59p.

"   : Le vrai "Combat" de Hitler ....
               Paris. L. Vogel. (1936) 317 p.

*ECKERT, Dietrich: Der Bolschewismus von Moses dis Lenin. Munchen,
     1925

*EICHEN, Dr. Carl von: Hitler' s Throat. Time Magazine, Nov. 14, 1938.

EINZIG, Paul: Hitler's "New Order" in Europe. London. Macmillan. 1941.
     147 p.

*[unreadable], Kurt von: Adolf Hitler und die Kommenden. Leipzig.
     V.R. Lindner (1932) 160 p.

*ENSOR, Robert Charles K.: Who Hitler is. Oxford Pamphlets. No. 20. 1939,
     32 p.

"   "   " : Herr Hitler's Self Disclosure
                    in "Mein Kampf". Oxford Pamphlets
                    No. 3 (1939)

ERCKNER, S.: Hitler's Conspiracy against Peace. London. Gollanz. 1937.
     288 p.

ERMARTH, Fritz: The New Germany (Washington, 1936)

FEDER, Gottfried: Was will Adolf Hitler? Munche. P.Eber. 1931.
     23 p.

*FARNSWORTH, Lawrence: Dictators and Democrats, New York,
     McBride...1941

FICKE, Karl: Auf dem Wege nach Canossa. Klausthal. Selbstverlag.
     1931 47 p.

FLANNER, Janet: An American In Paris. New York. Simon Schister
   (1940)

*FLANNERY, Harry W.: Assignment to Berlin. New York. 1942,
   430 p.

FODOR, M.W.: Plot and Counterplot in Central Europe. (Houghton)
   Boston, 1937, 317 p.

FOREIGN AFFAIRS: SCHEFFER, P.: Hitler Phenomenon and Portent.
   10:382-90, April, 1932.

FORUM - CLATCHIE, S.M.: Germany Awake. 85:217-24, April, 1931.

   "   OMBELL, H.D.: Dept. of brief Biography. Reply to mail Ludwig.
                             98 supp.10/11. December, 1937.

FRANCOIS, Jean: L'Aiffaire Rohm-Hitler. Les Oeuvres Libres. Paris.
   1938 v. 209. p. 5-142.

FRATECO (pseud.) : M. Hitlerá Dictateur. Trad. de l'allemand sur le manuscript,
   inedit. Paris. L'eglantine. 1933 275 p.

*FRIED, Hans, Ernest: The Guilt of the German Army, New York, Macmillan,
   1942   426 p.

*FROMMER: Blood and Banquets. New York. Harper Bros. 1942. 322 p.

*FRY, Michael: Hitler's Wonderland . London. Murray. 1934

*FUCHS, Martin: Showdown in Vienna. New York. Putnam's, 1939.
   311 p.

FUEHRER, Der.   in 100 Buchern. Wir lesen. may, 1939. p.1-16.

*GANZER, Karl, Rich.: ...Von Ringen Hitlers um das reich. 1929-33
   "ZEITGESCHICHTE VERLAG". Berlin, 1935.

GEHL, Walter: Der Deutsche [unreadable]. Breslau. Hirt. 1938, 172 p.

*GEORGES-ANQUETIL:...Hitler conduit la bal. Paris. Les editions de
   Lutece. 1939, 632 p.

*GERMAN FOREIGN OFFICE: The German White Paper. June 23, 1940.

GOEBBELS, Dr. Josef: Kampf um Berliná NSDAP. Munchen. 1934.

   "   : Vom Kaiserhof zur Reichskanzlei.
                               NSDAP. Munchen. 1934. 312 p.

GOLDING, Louis: Hitler Through the Ages. London. Soverign Books Ltd.
   1940

GOLLOMB, Joseph: Armies of Spies. New York. Macmillan, 1939, 213 p.

*GOOD HOUSEKEEPING: 109:30/1. October, 1939.
   ALLEN, J.: Directors of Destiny.

GOREL, Michael: Hitler sans masque.

GRAACH, Heinrich: Freiheitskampf..Saarlouis. Hanson Verlag.,
   1935 64 p.

GREENWOOD, H.: Hitler's First Year. London. 1934. The spectator
   booklet. No. 5

[unreadable], Albert: Inside Germany. New York. Dutton. 1939. 374 p.

Dissecting the Hitler Mind

*GRIMM, Alfred Max: Horoscope..Hitler. Toelz. Selbstverlag, 1925.

GRITZBACH, Erich: Hermann Goering...London, 1939.

*GROSS, Felix: Hitler's Girls, Guns and Gangsters. London, Hurst.
   1941, 320 p.

*[unreadable], Karl: Warum Hitler? .. Der Aufschwung, Deutsche
   Reihe, 1933.

GUMBEL, Emil Julius: Zwei Jehre Mord. (Kapp Putsch) 1921. Berlin
   Verlag Neues Vaterland. 63 p.

      "   "   " : Les crimes politiques en Allemagne.
                                  1919-21 Paris. Gallimard, 1931

*GUNTHER, John: Inside Europe. New York. Harper Bros., 1936. 470 p.

*   "   " : The High Cost of Hitler. London, Hamilton, 1939. 126 p.

*HAAKE, Heinz: Das Ehrenbuch des Fuehrers. NSDAP. 1933.

*HADAMOWSKY, Eugen: Hitler kampft um den Frieden Europas.
   NSDAP. 1936, 210 p.

HADELN, Hajo, Freiherr von: Von Wesen einer Nationalsozialistischen
   Weltgeschichte. Frankfut a.M.Osterreith, 1935, 56 p.

*HAFFNER, S.: Germany: Jeckyll and Hyde. New York, Dutton, 1941, 318 p.

HAGEN, Paul: Will Germany Crack? New York, 1942

HAMBLOCH, Ernest: Germany Rampant. London. Duckworth,
   1939 297 p.

*HANFSTAENGL, Ernst Franz: Hitler in der Karrikstur der Welt.
   Berlin. Verlag Braune Bucher, 1933. 174 p. (neue Folge: Tat gegen
   Tinte. Berlin. O.Rentsch, 1934. 176 p.)

*HANISCH, Reinhold: I was Hitler's buddy. The New Republic. April 5

*HINKEL, Hans/BLEY, Wulf: Kabinett Hitler. Verlag Deutsche Kulturwacht.
   Berlin, 1933 (?) 64 p.

Hitler: Ja, aber-was sagt Hitler Selbst? Ein Auswahl v.H. Passow, 1931

    "   : und die Deutsche Aufgabe. Zefit-und Streitfragen. Heft 1, 1933.

    "   's Wollen. Werner Siebart. NSDAP, 1935.

    "   : Against the World...New York. Worker' s Library Publ., 1935.

    "   :   The man. (London, 1935) Friends of Europe Publ. No. 34, p.1-21

    "   :   Acquarelle. NSDAP. (1936)

    "   calls this Living. London, 1939. 225 p.

    "   in Hamburg. Hamburg, 1939.

HOEPER, Wilhelm: Adolf Hitler, der Erzieher der Deutschen. Breslau,
   Hirt Verl.,1934, 179 p.

*HOFFMANN, Heinrich: Deutschlands Erwachen. 1924;

*   "   "   : Hitler, wie ihn Keiner Kennt. Berlin,
                              1932, 96 p.

```
    "                "           : Hitler in seinen Bergen. Berlin.
                                   Zeitgeschichte Verlag, (1935).

    "                "           : Hitler Abseits vom Alltag. Berlin,
                                   Zeitgeschichte Verlag, 1937.

    "                "           : Hitler in Italien. Munchen. Verlag
                                   Heinrich Hoffmann, (1938) 96 p.

    "                "           : Hitler in seiner Heimat. Berlin.
                                   Zeitgeschichte Verlag, (1938)

    "                "           : Hitler baut Grossdeutschland, 1938, 311 p.

    "                "           : Hitler befreit Sudetendeutschland.
                                   Berlin, Zeitgeschichte Verlag, 1938.

    "                "           : Hitler in Polen. Berlin, Zettgeschtichte
                                   Verlag,   1939, 48 p.
```

HOFFMAN, Heinrich: (cont)

Hitler in Nohmen. Berlin, Zeitgeschichte Verlag, 1939

*HOLBECK, K.: Kaiser, Kanzler, Kampfer. Leipzig. A. Hoffmann, 1933, 41 p

HOLT, John G.: Under the Swastika. (Chapel Hill, 1936)

*HOOVER, Calvin B.: Germany enters the Third Reich, New York, 1933.

*HUDDLESTON, Sisley: Im My Time. London. J. Cape (1938) 411 p.

HUSS, Pierre, J.: The Foe We Face. New York, Doubleday, 1942,   300 p.

HUTTON, Graham: Survey after Munich. Boston, 1939.

IL POPOLO D'ITALI: 7-5-29. Hitler: Un processo intentato...15-5-29.
    I diffamtori condamnati...

INDIAN REVUE, the: Chancellor Hitler (KK Sr. Iyengar) 34, vol. 246.

JONES, Enest J.: Hitler, the Jews and Communists. Sydney,1933.

JOSEPHSON, Matthew: Nazi Culture...The John Day Pamphlets, 1933,
    32 p.

*KEMP, T.D.Jr.: Adolph Hitler and the Nazis, New York, Cook, 1933,
    32 p.

[unreadable], Thoimas: France on Berlin Time, New York, Lippincott..
    1941, 312 p.

KING, Joseph: The German Revolution. London, 1933.

*KDOTZ, Helmut: The Berlin Diaries. London, 1935.

*KNICKERBOCKER, B.R.: Is Tomorrow Hitler's? New York, Reynal,
    1941, 382 p.

*KOEHLER, Hansjurgen: Inside Information. Pallas Publ. London, 1940
    269 p.

*   "   "   : Inside the Gestapo. Hitler's Shadows
                              over the World. Pallas Publ. Co., Ltd.
                              London, 1940.

*KOEHLER, Pauline: The Women lived in Hitler's House. Sheridan House.

KOERBER, Adolf-Victor von: Adolf Hitler, sein Loben und seine Reden. Munchen. E.Boepple., 1923, 112 p.

*KRAUSS, Helene: Des Fuehrers Jugendstatten..Wein Kuhne, 1936.

KREBS, Hans: Wir Sudetendeutsche, Berlin, Runge, 1937, 168.p

KREBS: (cont.) Sudentendeutschland Marschiert! Berlin, Osmer. 1939.

KRUEGER, Kurt MD: "Inside Hitler", New York, Avalon Press , 1941, 445 p

*LADIES HOME JOURNAL: Story of the Two Mustaches, 57:18, July, 1940.

LANDAU, Rom: Hitler's Paradise, London, Faber, 1941

*LANIA, Leo: Today We areBrothers, New York, 1942, 344 p..

*LASWELL, H.D.: Psychology of Hitlerism. Political Quaterly, vol. 4, 373-384.

 *LAURIE, Arthur Pillans: The Case for Germany, Berlin, 1939.

LEE, John Alexander: Hitler, The Auckland Serv. Print. 1940.

LEERS, Johann v.: Adolf Hitler. Leipzig, 1932, 96 p. (Manner und Machto)

*LEFEVRE, Henri: Hitler au pouvoir. Paris, Bureau d'Uditions, 1938, 87 p.

*LE GRIX, Francois: ..20 jours chez Hitler. Paris, Grassot, 1923.

*LENGYEL, Emil: Hitler, New York, 1932. 250 p.

*LESKE, Gottfried: I was a Nazi Flier, New York, Dialpress, 1941. 351 p

LEWIS, Wyndham: Hitler, London, Chatto & Windus, 1931, 202 p.

*   "   "   : The Hitler Cult, London, 1939, 267 p.

LICHTENBERGER, Henri: The Third Reich. New York. 1937.

LIFE: Adolf Hitler's Rise to Power, 9:61-67, August 19, 1940.

*LITERARY DIGEST: Misfire of the German Mussolini. 76:23, March 17, 1923

        "   "   : Hitler, Germany's Would-Be Mussolini. 107: 18/6,
                          October 11, 1930

        "   "   : Handsome Adolf, The Man without a Country. 107:34,
                          October 16,1930.

        "   "   : Dangerous Days in Europe. 107:14/5. October 25, 1930

        "   "   : Adolf Hitler States His Case. 111:15, Nov. 21, 1931.

        "   "   : Hitler's outstanding Outburst 111:10. Dec., 19 1931

        "   "   : Transformation of Adolf Hitler, 112:13/4, Jan. 9, 1932

LITERARY DIGEST: (cont.) Freud's Fears of Hitler, 113:15 Apr, 23, 1932

        "   "   : Hitler's Star still in the Ascendant. 113:12/3, 5/7/32

        "   "   : Hitler's shattered Dream of Dictatorship, 114:13/4
                          November 19, 1932.

        "   "   : Gregor Strasser, Big Hitlerite Rebel. 115:13, 1/28/33.

*   "   "   : When Hitler Hit the Ceiling. 115:30, February 18, 1933

     "   "   : Bewildering Magic of Fuehrer Hitler. 115:10/1, 5/13/33.

*   "   "   : Comic Aspects of Hitler's Career, 116:13, August 26, 1933.

*   "   "   : HIGH, S : The Man who leads Germany. 116:5, Oct. 21, 1933.

     "   "   : Chancellor-Reichsfuhrer. Watching his Step, 118:12,
                         August 18, ,1934.

     "   "   : Abbe Dinnet Gives His Views of Two Dictators. 118:18,
                         November 17, 1934.

     "   "   :They Stood out from the Crowd in 1934. 118:7, 12/29/34.

*   "   "   HIGH, Stanley: Hitler and the New Germany. Oct. 7, 1933.

*LITTEN, Irmgard: Beyond Tears, New York[, Alliance Book Corp., 1940, 325 p.

*LIVING AGE, GOETZ, F: How Hitler Failed, 320:595-99, March 29 1924.

     "   "   : From Six to Six Millions. 339:243-45, November, 1930.

*   "   "   WILTENBERG, W.von: Hadsome Adolf. 304:14/5, March 1931
                             Handsome Adolf, reply R. vonWINSTINGHAUSEN,
                             Living Age, 341:165/6, October, 1931

     "   "   UNRUH, Fritz v.: Hitler in Action, August, 1931, p. 551.

     "   "   HITLER, Adolf: TO Vistory and Freedom, National Socialism,
Labor Party, 342:24/5, March 1932.

     "   "   : Hitler speaks. 344:114-16, April, 1933.

     "   "   : Hitler and his Gang. 344:419-22,, June 22, 1933.

*   "   "   : W.W.C.: Hitler's Salad Days, 345:44-48, Sept., 1933.

LIVING AGE (cont.) HENRY, Ernst: The Man Behind Hitler. October, 1933, p. 117.

     "   "   : Why I Like Hitler. 349:303-6, December, 1935,
                             (Dr. K. Scharping.)

*   "   "   : MORRELL, S.: Hitler's Hiding Place,
                             352:485-8, August, 1937.

*   "   "   : YEATS-CROWN, F.: A Tory Looks at Hitler. 364:512-4,
                             August, 1938.

     "   "   : AGHA KHAN: Faith in Hitler, 355:299-302, December, 1938.

     "   "   : KORNEY: The Man Who made Hitler rich.
                             355:337-41, December, 1938.

     "   "   : Hitler's Palace in the Clouds on the
                             Top of the Kehlstein. 356:32/3, March, 1939.

*   "   "   : Men Whom Hitler Obeys   355:142-5, April, 1939.

*   "   "   : Hitler at 50. 356:451-3, June, 1939.

     "   "   : MANN, K: Cowboy Mentor of the Fuhrer, Karl May.
                             359:217-222, November, 1940.

*   "   "   : Hitler's Private Rabbit Warren.
                             Reichschancellery, 360:321. June, 1941.

*LOCHNER, Louis, P.: What about Germany? New York, Dodd, 1942, 395 p.

LOEWENSTEIN, Hubert Prinz zu: On Borrowed Peace, New York, 1942.

LOEWENSTEIN, Karl: Hitler's Germany, New York, Macmillan, 1936, 176 p.

LORANT, Stefan: I was Hitler's Prisoner, London, Gollancz, 1935, 318 p.

*LORIMER, Emily D.: What Hitler Wants, Penguin Book, 193'.

*LUCCHINI, Pierre : (Pierre Dominic pseud.) Deux jours chez Ludendorff.
    Paris, 1924.

*LUDECKE, Kurt Georg W. I Knew Hitler, New Tork, Scribner, 1937, 814 p.

*LUDWIG, Emil: Three Portraits; Hitler, Mussolini, Stalin.
    New York, 1940, 127 p.

LUDWIG, Emil: (cont.) The Germans. Boston, Little..1941, 509 p.

*LURKER, Otto: Hitler hinter Festungsmauern. Berlin, Mittler, 1933, 71 p.

MARION, Paul: Leur Combat ... Hitler. Paris. Fayard, 1939, 347 p.

MASON, John Browm: Hitler s First Foes.Minneapolis, 1936, 118 p.

*MASSIS, Henry: "Chefs", Paris, Plon., 1939.

MAUGHAN, Fred, Herbert: Lies as Allies; New York,
    Oxford University Press, 1941, 64 p.

MAUPAS, Jacques: Le Chancellier Hitler et les elections allemandes
    (Correspondant, 1933. R.S. tome 294, p. 835-863).

MELVILLE, Cecil F.: The Truth about the New Party. London, Wishart, 1931

*MEND, Hans: Adolf Hitler im Felde. Diessen, Huber. Verlag, 1931 192 p

MEYER, Adolf: Mit Hitler im Bayerischen Infanterie Regt.
    Neustadt. Aupperle Verlag, 1934, 109 p.

*MILLER, Douglas: You can't do business with Hitler!
    Boston, Little, 1941. 329 p.

*MITTEILUNGEN des Deutschvolkischen Turnvereins Urfahr;
    Adolf Hitler in Urfahr. Folge. 67.12.Jahrang. (Austria)

MOELIER van den Bruck: Das Dritte Reich. Hamburg.
    Hanseatisce Verlags Anstalt. 1931, 321 p.

MORVILLIERS, Roger: .. Face A Hitler et Mein Kampf. Sevres en vente
    chez l'auteyr. 1939.

*[unreadable], Edgar Ansell: Germany puts the Clock Back.
    New York, 1933. (London. Penguin Book, 1938)

*[unreadable], Lilian: Rip Tide of Aggression.
    New York, Morrow, 1942, 247 p.

MUHLEN, Norbert: Hitler's Magician, Schacht. London, 1938, 228 p.

*MURPHY, James Baumgardner: Adolf Hitler, the Drama of His Career.
    London, Chapman, 1934.

MAAB, Ingbert: Ist Hitler ein Christ? Munchen, Zeichenring Verlag,
    1931, 47 p.

*NATION: DENNY, C.: France and the German Counter-Revolution.
    116:295-7, March 14, 1923

"   : [unreadable], W.H.: Ten Years of Hitler, Hundres of
Goethe. 134:307-8, March 16, 1932.

"   RADER, K.: Hitler. 134:462-64, April 20, 1932.

"   VILLARD, O.G.: FOlly of Adolf Hitler. 136:392, April 12, 1933.

"   JASZI, O.: Hitler Myth, a forecast. 136:553/4, May, 1933

"   VILLARD, O.G.: Nazi Child-mind. 137:614, November 29, 1935.

"   [unreadable]L, E.: Hitler and the French press.
138:216-7, February 21, 1934.

"   VILLARD, O.G.: Hitler's [unreadable] and Gott.
139:110, August, 1934.

"   Can Hitler Be Trusted? 140:645 June 5, 1935

"   VILLARD, O.G.: Issues and Men. 143:395, Ootober 3, 1936.

"   Hitler goes to Home. 145:520, May 7, 1938.

NATIONALSOZIALISMUS, das wahre Gesicht des. Bund deutscher
   Kriegsteilnehmer, Magdeburg, 69 p.

*NATIONALSOZIALISTISCHE MORATSHEFTE" Jahreng, 327, vol.4, Heft 39.33

BUCH, Walter: Der Fuhrer, p. 248-51.

* "   : Vol. 5. Heft 46.34, P.2. ANACKER, H.: Ritter Tod und Teufel.
* "   : Vol. 3. Heft 32.32 ,p.511-13, CABALLERO, G.E.: Das
             Geheimnisdes Nationalsozialismus.

* " "   : Vol.5. Heft 54, p.846-9, Adolf Hitler, 1926 in Gera.

*NATIONALSOZIALISTISCHE MORATSHEFTE (cont.): Vol. 5.Heft 55, p.954-58.

LINKE: Wie der Modies den Hitler zum Schweigen brachte.

*"   " Vol. 5.Heft 54. Geschichten sus der KAMPFZEIT.

NAZI PRIMER, the: Official Handbook. New York, Harper, 1938.

NEUMANN, Franz L.: Behemoth. New York, Oxford University Press,
   1942, 532 p.

*NEW REPUBLIC: Is Hitler Crazy? 97:2/3. November, 1936.

"   "   :
JANISCH, R.: I was Hitler's Buddy. 98:239-42, 270-72, 297-300, April 5-19, 1939.

* "   "   : (Medicus) A Psychiatrist Looks at Hitler.
                           98:326-7, April 26, 1939.

NEWS WEEK: Nazis Protest Use of Baby Snapshot 3:31, March 3, 1934.

"   "   : Hitler and Mussolini Meet. 3:10-12, June 23, 1934.

"   "   : Hitler Tells How He Directed Merciless
                         Bloodstroke, 4:10-11, July 21, 1934.

"   "   : Hitler' s First Great Crisis. 3:34, June 30, 1934.

"   "   : Hitler at Bavarian Retreat. 5:12-3, March 2, 1935.

"   "   : Cocksure Dictator Takes Timid-Soul

Dissecting the Hitler Mind

Precautions. 5:16, April 6, 1935.

    "   "   : Reichsfuhrer..What Hitler Is ....
7:27, May 16, 1936.

*   "   "   : Hitler and Mussolini Put Their Heads Together.
10:11-13, October 4, 1937.

*   "   "   : Adolf Hitler's Roman Holiday...11:15-6,
May 16, 1938

*   "   "   : When Hitler Started. 13:22, February 6, 1939.

    "   "   : Adolf Hitler's Double. 13:43, March 13 1939.

*NEWS WEEK (cont.): Hitler Enthroned... 13:21, May 1, 193(?)

*   "   "   : To the Fuhrer, Hitler is Terrific.
19:42, June 22, 1942

    "   "   : Phony Fuhrer, Impersonator Dryden.
20:51-2, July 20, 1942

*NEW YORK TIMES: November 21, 12:1. Rise as Idol. 1922.

*   "   : December 14, 5:7, Mrs. Andre Blendt Aids Cause, 1922.

    "   : May 12, LLL.6:8:8.Hitler Wins Libel Suit in Munich....1929.

*   "   : October 15, 1930. Interview

    "   : May 2 12:4. Sincerity, praised by V.F. Ridder, 1933.

    "   : December 3.IV.2:2. Hitler Stories Told in Vienna, 1933.

*   "   : December 26, 17:6 Gives Rides and Overcoat to
Hitch-hikers, 1933.

    "   : March II, VI, 1934. Feature article.
Personality and Private Life: see Tolischus.

    "   : August 12, IV. 1:7, 1934.

*   "   : January 28. 6:3. Interviewed by Lord Allen of
[unreadable], 1935.

*   "   : September 17, 4:4. Alois Hitler Opens Tea Room
in Berlin, 1937.

*   "   : September 19, IV.2:3. Portrait Adolf Hitler, 1937.

*   "   : April 16, 6:3. Gruenscheder says He is Older than
Record Show, 1938.

*   "   : March 31. 2:3 Relatives visit U.S.: William Patrick, 1939.

*   "   : October 6 10:4 Miss Daniels Interview on her dance
performance before him, 1939.

*   "   : November 17, VIII. 2:4. Report to have sought
Dr. Stekel to interpret dream of undisclosed nature, 1940.

NEW YORK TIMES (cont.)
: Januaary 3, 9:1 January 4. 9:2, January 7 (?):6. Reports
about arrival of U. Freeman Mitford - illnes in England, 1940.

    "   : January 26. 2:2 German Official (?) Honduran Foreign
Office to ban book, "I was Hitler's Waitress", 1941

" : June 30, 5:3 and June 25, 4:3. Reports about William
Patrick and Mrs. Bridget arrivals, activities in Canada
and U.S., 1941

NEW YORK TIMES MAGAZINE:

" TOLISCHUS; Portrait of a Revolutionary, p.3, May 19, 1940.

" PETERS, C.B.: In Hitler's Chalet. p. 9, 3/16/41.

NEW YORKER STAATSZEITUNG und Herold.:
   Various articles. April, 1939; December 1940.

*" [unreadable] aus Privatleben. Preston Grover, January 2, 1941.

NIEKISCH, Ernst: Hitler-Ein Deutsches Vergaengnis. Berlin. Widerstands
   Verlag, 1932.

*NINETEENTH CENTURY: WILXON, Sir Arnold: October, 1936. p.503-512.

NORTH AMERICAN REVUE: Herr Hitler come to Bat. 1932, 234, vol. 104-9

*OESCNSNER, Frederick: This is the Enemy. Boston, Little, 1942, 364 p.

[unreadable], Walter: Kommt gas Dritte Reich? Berlin, Rowohlt, 1930.

*OLDEN, Rudolph: Hitler, Amsterdam, Queride, 1935, 364 p.

*OTTO, Carol A.G.: Der Krieg ohne Waffen. Wird Hitler Deutschlands
   Mussolini. Sanitas Verlag, 1930, 69 p.

OTTWALT, ERNST: Deutschland Erwache! Vienna, 1832, Hess & Co.

[unreadable], Frank: The Three Dictators...Hitler. London, Allen, 1940.

OUTLOOK: BINEES, H.L.: Hitler, German Hypnotist, 156, vol. 266, 1931.

*PARISER TAGES ZEITUNG: April 20, 1937. Das Ratsel um Hitlers, E.K.I.

* "   "   "   : Jan. 28, 1939. Der Prozess der Brigette Hitler.

* "   "   "   : Sept. 29, 1939. Article about the Iron Cross.

* "   "   "   : Jan. 23, 1940. Vom [unreasonable]

PASCAL, Roy: The Nazi Dictatorship. London, 1934.

*PAOLI, Ernst: Die Sendung Adolf Hitlers. Verlag fur Volkskunst, 1934.

*PAULS, Eilhard, Erich: Ein Jahr Volkskanzler. (Aus Deutchlands Verden,
   Heft 21/1. 1934, 31 p.)

PERNOT, Maurice: L'Allemagne de Hitler, Paris, 1933

*PHILLIPS, Henry Albert: Germaany Today and Tomorrow, New York, Dodd.

*PICTORIAL REVIEW: RADZIWELL, C/ZIENKORSCH, T.v.: Three Women Behind
   the Demogogue, 34:7, July 1933.

*PLESSMAYR, Hermann: Der Nationalsocizlismus...
   Stuttgart, Mahler, 1933, 104 p.

POLLOCK, James Kerr: The Government of Greater Germany, New York,
   Nostrand, 1932, 104 p.

*POPE, Ernest R.: Munich Playground, New York, Putnam's, 1941, 260 p.

Dissecting the Hitler Mind

[unreadable], Walther: Hitler.Langensalza. 1934 (Heft, 1931 v.
   Friedr. [unreadable], p. 1-41).

[unreadable], Karl: Jitler-Entwicklungsmoglichkeiten. Oxford, 1933,
   vol. 14, p. 450-54. Blackfriars.

*PRICE, George Ward: I Knew These Dictators. London, Harran, 1937, 262 p.

*RALEIGH, Jogn McCutcheon: Behind the Nazi Front.
   New York, Dodd, 1940, 307 p.

RAUSCHNING, Anna: No Retreat. New York, Bobbs Merrill, 1942, 309 p.

*RAUSCHNING, Herman: The Voice of Destruction same as "Gesprache mit Hitler".

*   "   "   : The Revolution of Nihilisme. New York,
                           Alliance Book Corp., 1939, 300 p.

*   "   "   : Gesprache mit Hitler. New York, Europa
                           Verlag, 1940, 272 p.

    "   "   : Hitler and the War. American Council on Public
                           Affairs, 1940, 11p.

    "   "   : The Conservative Revolution. New York, Putnam's,
                           1941, 280 p.

    "   "   : The Beast From the Abyss- London, Heinemann,
                           1941, 170 p.

*   "   "   : Men of Chaos, New York, Putnam's, 1942, 341 p.

READER'S DIGEST: SPIWAK, J.L.: Hitler' s Racketeers, 28:52-4, MARCH, 1936.

REICH, ALBERT: AUS ADOLF HITLERS NEIMST. 1933, 128 P.

*REVEILLE, Thomas (pseud.) The Spoil of Europe, New York, Norton, 1941, 344 p.

REVUE [unreadable]: Vingt jours chez Hitler. (F.LeGrix), Paris,
   42 A.4. 94-118.5 84-98.

*REYNOLDS, Bernard Talbot: Prelude to Hitler. London, J.Cape, 1933, 288 p.

RIBBENTROP, Manfred v.: Um den Fuhrer (Volkische Reihe im Winterverlag
   Heft 1) 1933, 32 p.

*REISS, Curt: The Self-Betrayed. Putnam's, New York, 1942, 402.

*RITTER, Walther: Adolf Hitler.. Leipzig. Verlag Nationalsoz Front, 1933, 32 p.

ROBERT, Karl: (pseud.) Hitler's Counterfeit Reich. New York,
   Alliance Book Corp. 1941, 122.

*ROBERTS, Stephen H.: The House that Hitler Built. New York, 1938, 364 p.

*ROCH, Hans: Gott segne den Kanzler. 20.April 1933. 11 p. Reendfunkrede.

*ROEM, Ernert: Die Geschichte eines Hochverrators.
   Munchen, F. Eber, 1933, 367 p.

ROGGE, Heinrich: Hitler's Friedenspolitik..Berlin. Schlieffen. 1936, 127 p.

ROPER, Edith (und Clara Leiser): Sceleton of Justice, New York,
   Dutton, 1941. 246 p.

*SANTORO, Cesare: Hitler Deutschland...Berlin. Inter.Nat. Verl, 1938.

*   "   "   : Vier Jahre Hitlerdeutschland..1937.

*SATURDAY EVENING POST: -SONDERNm F.Jr.: Schuschnigg's terrible two hours.
211:23. August 13, 1938.

*   "   "   "   : [unreadable], R.: Is Hitler Married? 12:14/5.
December 16, 1939 ..

"   "   "   : [unreadable], H.: We Blundered Hitler into
Power 213:12/3, July 13, 1940.

*   "   "   "   : McKELWAY, St. C.: Who Was Hitler? 213:12, July 20, 1940.

"   "   "   : WALDECKK, Countess: Girls Did Well under Hitler,
215:18, September 2O, 1942.

SATURDAY REVIEW (of London): [unreadable]: A German View of Hitler,
153 vol. 314/5, 1932.

"   "   : MAXWELL, N.: Hitler's He Men and the Cash.
156 vol, 142, 1933.

SATURDAY REVIEW OF LITERATURE:
BAKER, J.E.: Carlyle Rules the Reich. 10:291, November 25, 1933

SATURDAY REVIEW OF LITERATURE (cont.)
JOSEPHSON, M.: Making of a Demagogue. 10:213/4. Oct. 28, 1933.

*SCHACHER, Gerhard: He Wanted to Sleep in the Kremlin. New York,
1942. 261 p.

SCHEID,, O.: Les Memoires de Hitler. Paris, Perrin, 1933.

*SCHIRACH, Baldur v.: Die Pioniere des Dritten Reichs. Essen, 1933

*SCHMIDT-PAULI, Edgar v.: Hitlers Kampf um die Mecht. Berlin, 1933, 205 p.

*   "   "   "   : Die Manner um Hitler Verlag fur Kulturpolitik,
Berlin, 1932 (Neue erganzte Ausgabe, 1935, 190 p.)

*   "   "   "   : Adolf Hitler, Berlin, De VO Verlag, 1934, 126 p.

SCHOLASTIC; Hitler Crushes Foes...25:15. September 22, 1934.

*SCHOTT, Georg: Das Volksbuch vom Hitler. Munchen. Eber. 1933, 307 p.

SCHRAEDER, Fred Franklin: The New Germany....New York. Deutscher
Weckruf & Beobachter. 1937

*SCHROEDER, Arno: Hitler [unreadable] auf die Dorffer.
National. Soz. Verlag,   1938, 21 2 p.

*SCHULTZE-PFAELZER, Gerhard: Hindenburg und Hitler.
Berlin, Stollberg, 1933, 96 p.

*SCHULZE, Kurt: Adolf Hitler, London, Harrap, 1935, 80 p.

SCHWARZCHILD, Leopold: World in Trance, New York, 1942, 445 p.

SCIENCE NEWS LETTER: LASWELL, H.D.: Hitler Rose to Power
Because he Felt Personally Insecure. 33:195. March 26, 1938.

"   "   "   : Hitler's Personality Called Paranoid,
infantile, sadistic. 34:227/8, October 8, 1938.

*SCHRIBNER, W.D.: Hail Hitler! M.9:229-31, April, 1932

SCYLER, J.P.: Hitler et son troisteme empire. Paris, L'Eglantine, 1933.

*[unreadable], Herbert: Mit dem Fuhrer [unreadable] NSDAP, 1939, 228 p.

[unreadable], Toni: A Fighter for Peace. New York, Vanguard, 1939

*SHIRER, William L.: Berlin Diary, New York, Knopf. 1941, 605 p.

*SHUSTER, George N.: Strong Man Rules. (New York, 1934)

*SIMONE, Andre: Men of Europe. New York, Moder Age, 1941, 330 p.

*SMITH, Howard K.: Last Train from Berlin. New York. 1932, 359 p.

*SNYDER, Louis: Hitlerism...by Nordicus (pseud.) New York, Mohawk Press, 1932.

SPENCER, Franz: Battles of a Bystander. New York, Liveright, 1941, 260 p.

*[unreadable], Ernst, [unreadable]: Prinz: Between Hitler and
  Mussolini. London, Hodder...1942. 281 p.

STARK, Johannes: Adolf Hitlers Ziele...Deutscher Volksverlag, 1930, 32 p.

STATIST, the: Hitler's Day. London, 1934, 123 vol. 181.

STEED, Henry Wickham: Hitler Whence and Whither? London, [unreadable],
  1934, 189 p.

STREL, Johnnes: Hitler ale Frankenstein. London, 1933, 185 p.

*STEYRER ZEITUNG: Aldof Hitler als Schuler in Steyr. April 17, 1938.

*STODDARD, Lothrop: Into the Darkness. New York. Duell, 1940, 311 p.

STRASSER, Otto: aufbau des deutschen Sozialismus. Prag.I. Heinrich
  Grunow, 1936.

* "   " : Hitler and I. Boston, Houghton, 1940, 248 p.

  "   " : Free Germany Against Hitler, Brooklyn, N.Y., 1941, 15 p.

*STRASSER, Otto: (cont.)
              Die deutsche Bartholomausnacht. Zurich,
              Reso Verlag, 1935, 242 p.

* "   "   : Flight from Terro.

[unreadable], Gustav: Letters and Diaries. London, Macmillan, 1935-40.

SURVEY, the: (J.P.Gavit) Much ado about Hitler. 68 vol. 239.

TACITUS REDIVIVUS (pseud.) Die Grosse Trommel. 155 p.

*TAGEBUCH, das: -TSCHUPPIK, Karl: Jitler spricht. 498, 1927

  "   " :   -SCHER, Pet.: Hitlergesandter bei Ford. VII. 628, 1928.

* "   " :   -REIDEN, K.: Hitler klagt. X.816, 1929

  "   " :   -SCHWARZSCHILD, L.: Ave Adolf: XII, 1808. (1931).

*TAT, die: ROTHE, M." Siegesallee II, (A. Hitler(21.J.780-4

TAYLOR, Edmond: The Strategy of Terror. Boston, Houghton,
  1940. 277 p. (1942 revised edition)

*TEELING, William: Know Thy Enemy! London, Nicholson, 1939, 313 p.

TENNANT, E.W.D.: Herr Hitler and his Policy, March 1933.
  English Review v. 56. p 362, 375.

TESSON, Francois de: Voici Adolf Hitler. Paris. Flammarion, 1936, 284 p.

THYSSEN, F.: I made a Mistake When I Backed Hitler. American
   Magazine, 1930: 16-7. July, 1940.

*   "   : I Paid Hitler. New York, Farrar, 1941, 281 p.

*THOMPSON, Dorothy: I Saw Hitler, New York, 1932.

*TIME: Let's Be Friends! 27:21-2, March 9, 1936.

   "   Critic Hitler, 30. August 2, 1937 (p. 32-A.2)

   "   Hitler Comes Home. 31:18-22, March 21, 1938.

   "   Hitler's Throat. 32:55. November 14, 1938.

   "   Man of the Year. 33:11-14. January 2, 1939/

   "   Office and Official Residence...33:17/8. January 23, 1939.

TIME: (cont.) Fuehrer's Next.. 33:22 March 13, 1939.

*   "   : Hitler vs. Hitler, 33:20, April 10, 1939.

*   "   : Aggranndizer's Anniversary, 33:23/4, May 1, 1939

   "   : Two Diagnoses, 33:22, May 8, 193(?)

   "   : Eleven Minutes; Hitler's Narrow Escape   34:21/2,
           November 20, 1939

   "   : Mississippi Frontier, [unreadable] Wiegand's
           Interview, 35:37-8, June 20, 1940

*   "   : Happy Hitler. 36:18, July 15, 1940.

   "   : Hitler Takes a Trip. 36:28, Nov. 4, 1940.

   "   : Orator Hitler. 37:19, Jan. 13, 1941.

*   "   : Dictator's Hour. 37:26-8 April 14, 1941.

   "   : Happy Birthday. 37:22/3. April 28, 1941.

   "   : Inside Hitler. 39:43, June 22, 1942.

*TOLISCHUS, Otto D.: They Wanted War. New York, Reynolds, 1940, 340 p.

*TOURLEY, Robert (et Z. Lvovsky): Hitler. Paris, Editions due
   siecle. 1932, 200 p.

*TROSSMAN, Karl: Hitler und Rom.Nurnberg.Sebaldus Verlag, 1931.

TROTZKY, Leon: What Hitler Wants. New York, John Bay Go., 1933, 31 p.

   "   "   : How Long Can Hitler Stay? (American Mercury v. 31.
               p. 1-17), 1934

TURNER, James: Hitler and the Empire. London, 1937, 40 p.

VERGES, Ferni: El [unreadable] abans de Hitler. Revista de
   Catalunya. 1938. juny 15, p. 213-225)

VIE deI Peuples, Adolf Hit]er. Annee 4, p. 536-44, Paris, 1923.

*VOIGT, F,A.: Unto Caesar New York. Putnam's, 1938, 303 p.

VORWAERTS: GOETZ, F.: Ein Offizer Hitlers erzahlt. 3.2.24.
*   "   "   : Report on Putsch Prozess. February 26, 1924.

*WHO, JACOB, Hans: Hitler's Ear and Tongue. Vol. 1. No. 2., I,iay, 1941,
    p. 37-8

*WEIGAND, Karl v.: Hitler Foresees His End. Cosmopolitan,
    April, 1939, p.28.ff and May p.48 ff.

WILD, Alfons: Hitler und das Christentum. Augsburg. Hass., 1931, 85 p.

WIR fliegen mit Hitler. Berlin. Deutsche Kulturwacht, 1934, 184 p.

WOLF, John: Nazi Germany. London, 1934.

WYL, Hans von: Ein Schweizer erlebt Deutschland. Zurich, Europa Verlag, 1938.

*YOUNG, William Russel: Berlin Embassy, 1941, 280 p.

*ZIEMER, Gregor: Education for Death, New York, Oxford University
    Press,1941, 208 p.

CPSIA information can be obtained at www.ICGtesting.com

262807BV00005B/68/P

9 780984 158409